EDUCATION

AND THE

DEMOCRATIC

IDEAL

EDUCATION

AND THE

DEMOCRATIC

IDEAL

STEVEN M. CAHN

NELSON-HALL

nh

CHICAGO

Books by Steven M. Cahn

Education and the Democratic Ideal
The Eclipse of Excellence
A New Introduction to Philosophy
Fate, Logic, and Time

Books Edited by Steven M. Cahn

Scholars Who Teach: The Art of College Teaching
New Studies in the Philosophy of John Dewey
Classics of Western Philosophy
Philosophy of Religion
The Philosophical Foundations of Education
Philosophy of Art and Aesthetics: From Plato to
  Wittgenstein (co-editor)

Library of Congress Cataloging in Publication Data

Cahn, Steven M
  Education and the democratic ideal.

  Bibliography: p.
  Includes index.
  1. Education, Higher—Aims and objectives.
  2. College teaching.   3. Universities and colleges—
  Examinations. I. Title.
  LB2324.C33   378'.01   78-27155
  ISBN 0-88229-589-6

Manufactured in the United States of America

10   9   8   7   6   5   4   3   2   1

To my mother
EVELYN BAUM CAHN
the finest teacher I have ever known

Contents

Preface

This book amplifies and unifies my previously published writings concerning American higher education. In particular, it builds upon material that first appeared in my brief work *The Eclipse of Excellence*, and I thank its publisher, Public Affairs Press, for permission to reprint segments.

My wife, Marilyn, has been a constant source of support and encouragement. And I am grateful as always to my brother, Victor, my trusted guide on matters literary and otherwise.

The volume is dedicated to my mother, who for many years taught English, as well as American history and German, at Thomas Jefferson High School in Elizabeth, New Jersey. Her profound understanding of the process of education has shaped my outlook on learning and life.

Introduction

In Lewis Carroll's *Alice's Adventures in Wonderland*, the heroine, lost in the woods, comes upon a grinning Cheshire Cat sitting on a bough of a tree.

"Cheshire Puss," she began, rather timidly, as she did not at all know whether it would like the name: however, it only grinned a little wider. . . . "Would you tell me, please, which way I ought to go from here?"

"That depends a good deal on where you want to get to," said the Cat.

"I don't much care where—" said Alice.

"Then it doesn't matter which way you go," said the Cat.

"—so long as I get *somewhere*," Alice added as an explanation.

"Oh, you're sure to do that," said the Cat, "if you only walk long enough."[1]

This exchange is an appropriate starting point
for reflection upon higher education in America today, for while everyone seems to be anxiously won-
dering which steps ought to be taken, few seem to
have decided just where those steps ought to lead. Of
course, as the Cheshire Cat reminded Alice, whatever we do we are sure to get somewhere; but, as he
mischievously failed to remark, we may well be unhappy when we arrive at our destination.

Thus our present predicament. Without careful
examination of the aims of education, debate rages
over numerous controversies: Should grades be
abolished? Are off-campus experiences suitable for
academic credit? What role should students play in
the evaluation of their teachers? Is it wise to require
study of a foreign language? But reasonable answers
to any of these or similar questions require prior
consideration of educational goals. What sense is
there, for example, in supporting or opposing a
foreign language requirement without first determining why foreign languages should be taught at
all? How can we responsibly adopt or reject changes
in grading practices before clarifying the purposes
grades are supposed to serve?

Admittedly, discussion of the aims of education
inevitably proves more abstract and frequently appears far duller than debate over some flashy meth-
odological novelty. But methods are adopted to
achieve goals, and if our goals are ill-chosen, we must
rethink our methods. For that reason, questions of
procedure are inseparable from questions of purpose.

Failure to observe this principle accounts for
much of the confusion presently pervading our colleges and universities. We are engulfed by an abundance of techniques but suffer from a paucity of planning. We eagerly embrace any idea hailed as an

innovation, although rarely can we say exactly what we are thereby trying to accomplish. Entire schools have even been founded on nothing more than a commitment to continual change, despite the obvious fact that change is not always progress and sometimes leads to disaster.

The time has come to cease our frantic dashes this way and that; we must stop and think where we should be headed. In other words, we need to reexamine our aims, to formulate them clearly, to systematize them, and to render them explicit by considering how we might implement them.

That is the enterprise I shall attempt in this book: the presentation of a coherent, thorough, and sound philosophy of higher education. With this philosophy in hand, we shall know where we want to go, and we can choose intelligently those traditions and those innovations that together will enable us to approach the fulfillment of our goals.

Chapter 1

The Democratic Framework

Education is the acquisition of knowledge, skills, and values. But what knowledge, skills, and values ought to be acquired? Who ought to acquire them? And how should they be acquired? These questions highlight the three central concerns of any philosophy of education: the subject matter, the student, and the instructional method. And primary among these is the student, for what is to be learned and how it is to be learned ultimately depend upon who is to do the learning.

Here is where our educational philosophy rests on our political philosophy, for a commitment to the democratic system of government implies a concern for the education of every citizen. In a democracy our own welfare depends heavily upon the wisdom of our neighbors. To some this claim may appear no more than naïve sentimentality, but dismissing it as such would be a fundamental error, a misunderstanding of the processes of decision-making within a democratic society.

Perhaps no setting better exemplifies the essence of democracy than a polling place on election day. There, waiting to cast ballots, are the various members of the community—the carpenter, the waitress, the lawyer, the bus driver, the street cleaner, the businessman, the piano tuner, the nurse. Each is given one vote, and the will of the majority prevails.

Standing in line right behind one another, we might imagine, are Archie Bunker and a professor of political science. If asked about his preferences, Archie might reply that he doesn't have any idea who's running in this election, but that it doesn't make any difference anyway, since he has voted for the same party all his life and has no intention of ever switching. As for the bond issue that appears in the upper-right-hand corner of the voting machine, he hadn't realized it was there, but now that you've mentioned it, he will be sure to vote against it, since he votes against all bond issues on the grounds that he prefers things just as they are and doesn't care for any changes. (If Archie seems too much a caricature, consider how important a candidate deems the exact position of his name on the ballot. Politicians are well aware that the top spot is preferable, since a sizable number of voters select whichever is the first name on the list, apparently believing that higher is better.)

Standing behind Archie is a university professor who has devoted his life to an intense study of the American political system. He may be familiar with the views of every candidate on the ballot and may even have helped formulate the exact wording of the bond issue. He, like Archie, receives one and only one vote. His erudition entitles him to nothing more.

Does this system make any sense? After all, if you visited a physician and sought advice as to whether to undergo an operation, you would be appalled if he explained that his policy in such cases was to poll a random sampling of passersby and act in accordance with the will of the majority. A community would be similarly dismayed if it hired an engineer to build a bridge, and he appeared one day to announce that he could not decide how deeply to lay the foundations and would like to be guided by a vote of the townspeople. To solve medical or engineering problems, we seek expert judgment, not the uninformed opinions of the populace. Why, then, faced with political problems, do we take the issue to all the people, rather than to a specialist?

Plato asked this question in his *Republic*, and, believing there to be no reasonable answer, he proceeded to construct a system of government based on the view that issues of public policy, being complex, technical matters, ought to be placed in the hands of experts. The Platonic utopia was to be directed and controlled by a small group of philosopher-kings, chosen on the basis of their natural aptitudes and specially educated for their role. Most members of that society were to be mere tradesmen; the farmer was expected only to farm, the cobbler only to cobble. They were to play no role in the governance of the state, and their education, therefore, was to be in the narrowest sense a trade education. Indeed, from Plato's point of view, it would have been a grave mistake even to suggest to a farmer or cobbler that he participate in the affairs of government, for the farmer was naturally fitted only to farm, the cobbler naturally fitted only to cobble. The philosopher-kings

were the individuals naturally fitted to rule, and they
would do so most effectively if not interfered with by
those ill-suited to deliberate about the important decisions affecting the future of their society.

Plato compared the working of a democratic society to the situation aboard a ship on which the sailors
are arguing over the control of the helm, while none
of them has ever learnt navigation. And if someone
on board happens to possess the needed skills, his
qualifications are disregarded on the grounds that
steering a ship requires no special competence. Plato
scornfully observed that ". . . with a magnificent
indifference to the sort of life a man has led before he
enters politics . . . [a democracy] will promote to
honour anyone who merely calls himself the people's
friend."[1]

Even the most ardent supporter of the democratic form of government must recognize the force of
Plato's trenchant criticisms. But an intelligent commitment to democracy is not based upon a belief in the
system's perfection, for no human institution is infallible. The question is not whether democracy has
weaknesses; the question is whether democracy has
fewer weaknesses than any of the alternatives. And
here, I believe, is where Plato's analysis went awry.

By whatever procedures the rulers of an oligarchy are selected, mistakes are possible, and, as the
events of history have so often demonstrated, once
unrestrained authority is placed in the wrong hands,
the results are calamitous. In a democracy the foolish
decision made on one occasion can be undone on
another, but when all control has been transferred to
the oligarchs, second chances are no longer possible.
Members of a democracy avoid having to make the
difficult, dangerous, and unalterable decision of
whom to entrust with absolute power.

Furthermore, however kindhearted the rulers

may initially appear, in time they tend to lose touch with those they rule, and even the best-intentioned of sovereigns find it difficult to remain sensitive to the needs and desires of those under their control. Lord Acton's aphorism remains applicable: "Power tends to corrupt; absolute power corrupts absolutely." Faced with debased leadership, citizens of a democracy can vote improvement, but citizens of an oligarchy must either shed their own blood in attempted revolution or else suffer in silence.

Although oligarchs may possess greater expertise in certain technical matters than do other individuals, each member of a society possesses special insight into his own problems, interests, and goals. John Dewey pointed out that "the individuals of the submerged mass may not be very wise. But there is one thing they are wiser about than anybody else can be, and that is where the shoe pinches, the troubles they suffer from."[2] Only the democratic system ensures that this self-knowledge is taken into account in the governmental process.

A democratic society is distinguished, moreover, by the quality of life inherent in its procedures. Competitive elections require the expression of opposing points of view, the protection of the right of citizens to speak freely, to write freely, to assemble freely. The open air of a democracy invites individuality and variety, thereby enhancing the opportunity for increased self-consciousness and self-fulfillment. Conflicting ideas and attitudes produce a vitality that enriches the experience of all.

However, now having made the case for democracy, we should consider the potential weaknesses of the system. It is fine to have faith in the common man, but anyone who realizes the tragic mistakes and gross injustices that have been carried out in accordance with the will of the majority knows how foolish or immoral popularly supported policies can be. And the responsibility for such failures must ultimately be borne by the members of a democracy themselves. No matter how angrily they may denounce their political leaders, the people originally chose them and can by the very same process replace them. Every elected official is aware that in order to retain his position he must be sensitive to the desires of his constituents; if he is out of touch with their wishes, he will soon be forced to seek other employment.

But this power of the people presents democracy with its most crucial problem, for what defense is there against a narrow-minded or gullible citizenry? If the public cannot distinguish reason from demagogy, integrity from duplicity, wisdom from folly, then all is lost. For not only is an open society susceptible to a misguided majority, but by its very nature it offers avenues to power for potential tyrants who, having availed themselves of freedom, would at the first opportunity deny it to others.

So the crucial question is: how can the members of a democracy be provided with the necessary understanding and capability to reap the greatest possible benefits from the democratic process while at the same time protecting that process from those who would seek its destruction? The answer is to be found in the enterprise of education.

Now it becomes clear why in a democracy every individual's education should be of such vital concern. For the ignorance of some is a threat to all. If a person should complain that his democracy is providing too much education for too many people, he thereby reveals his misunderstanding of the nature of a democratic society. How can the electorate be too educated, how can they know too much, how can they be too astute? Too little education, however, and there may soon be no democracy.

Chapter 2

The Content of a
Liberal Education

Having recognized the need for education within a democracy, we need to determine the appropriate content of that education. In addition to an understanding and appreciation of the democratic system itself, what knowledge, skills, and values are necessary to enable individuals to live intelligently and responsibly as free persons in a free society?

We may begin by noting the obvious fact that all members of a democracy should be able to read, write, and speak effectively. An individual who is unable to understand others or make himself understood is both hindered in his personal growth and unable to participate fully in the free exchange of opinions so vital to the democratic process. A command of language is indispensable in the marketplace of ideas, and hence it is of vital importance for members of a democracy to acquire linguistic facility.

Also essential is an understanding of public issues. How can a citizen sensibly enter into discussion of matters he does not understand? How can he reasonably evaluate the judgment of his representatives if he is unable to comprehend the complexities of the questions they are deciding? In a democracy public issues cover an enormous range of topics, for every action of a government is an appropriate subject for open discussion, and such actions typically involve social, political, economic, scientific, and historical factors. Consider some of the critical issues confronting the world today: poverty, overpopulation, pollution, ideological conflict, the dangers of nuclear warfare, and the possible benefits of space research. How can these matters be intelligently discussed or even understood by those ignorant of the physical structure of the world, the forces that shape society, or the ideas and events that form the background of present crises? Thus substantial knowledge of natural science, social science, world history, and national history is required for all those called upon to think about public issues, and in a democracy such participation is required of everyone. Granted, elected representatives must carry the major burden of formulating and implementing governmental policies. Still, each citizen has both the right and the duty to evaluate and try to influence the decisions of his government.

The study of science requires familiarity with the fundamental concepts and techniques of mathematics, since such notions play a critical role in the natural sciences and an ever increasing role in the social sciences. Furthermore, apart from its use in other inquiries, mathematics is itself an invaluable aid in the handling of everyday affairs, for, as Alfred

North Whitehead noted: "Through and through the world is infected with quantity. To talk sense, is to talk in quantities. It is no use saying the nation is large,—How large? It is no use saying that radium is scarce,—How scarce? You cannot evade quantity."[1]

But to know the results of scientific and historical investigations is not sufficient; one must also understand the methods of inquiry that have produced those results. No amount of knowledge brings intellectual sophistication, unless one also possesses the power of critical thinking. To think critically is to think in accord with the canons of logic and scientific method, and such thinking provides needed protection against the lure of simplistic dogmas that appear attractive, yet threaten to cut the lifeline of reason and stifle the intellect. A member of a democracy who cannot spot a fallacious argument or recognize relevant evidence for a hypothesis is defenseless against those who would twist facts to suit their own purpose.

Still another characteristic should be possessed by all members of a democracy: sensitivity to aesthetic experience. An appreciation and understanding of the literature, art, and music of various cultures enriches the imagination, refines the sensibilities, deepens feelings, and provides increased awareness of the world in which we live. In a society of aesthetic illiterates not only the quality of art suffers but also the quality of life.

In connection with the study of literature it should be noted that significant value is derived from reading some foreign literature in its original language. Not only does great literature lose some of its richness in translation, but learning another language increases linguistic sensitivity and makes one more conscious of the unique potentialities and limitations of any particular tongue. Such study is also a most effective means of widening cultural horizons, for understanding another language is a key to understanding another culture.

Another indispensable element of education for members of a democracy is a knowledge of human values. Aristotle long ago recognized that virtue is of two kinds, what he termed "moral virtue" and "intellectual virtue." Moral virtue, which we might call "character," is formed by habit. One becomes good by doing good. Repeated acts of justice and self-control result in a just, self-controlled person who not only performs such acts but does so from an unshakeable disposition.

Intellectual virtue is what we might refer to as "wisdom." In a narrow sense, a wise person is one who is a good judge of value. He can distinguish worth from cost. He is blessed with discernment, discretion, and an abundance of that most precious of qualities, common sense.

But in a broader sense, a wise person is one with intellectual perspective, who is familiar with both the foundations of knowledge and its heights, who can scrutinize the fundamental principles of thought and action while maintaining a view of the world that encompasses both what is and what ought to be. The path to wisdom in this sense lies in the study of those subtle analyses and grand visions that comprise philosophy. Such understanding affords a defense against intimidation by dogmatism while providing a framework for the operation of intelligence.

Clearly, education within a democracy must not be limited to training individuals in occupational techniques, for regardless of a citizen's mode of employment, he is expected to make judgments about sundry matters of public policy, and his education must be broad enough to enable him to do so wisely. Among the Romans such an education was permitted only to freemen (in Latin: *liberi*), and we thus refer to it as a "liberal education."

It would be a serious error, however, to separate liberal and vocational education. If the members of a democracy are to be not only knowledgeable participants in the political arena but also effective contributors in the social sphere, each should be provided with the necessary skills, social orientation, and intellectual perspective to succeed in some wide field of occupational endeavor. But such vocational education must not be confused with narrow job-training. Animals are broken in and trained; human beings ought to be enlightened and educated. An individual ignorant of the aims of his actions is unable to adjust in the face of changing conditions and is thus stymied by a world in flux. Sidney Hook has observed: "There is a paradox connected with vocational training. The more vocational it is, the narrower it is; the narrower it is, the less likely it is to serve usefully in earning a living . . . there is no reason—except unfamiliarity with the idea—why vocational education should not be liberalized to include the study of social, economic, historical, and ethical questions. . . ."[2] Such broadened vocational preparation is not only of use to the future worker himself; its benefit to society is apparent to anyone who has ever been forced to deal with the mechanized mind of a bureaucrat.

As a means of further clarifying the content of a liberal education, consider the oft-repeated objection that such an education is not relevant. What is the appropriate reply?

Sometimes "relevant" is taken to mean "topical." In this sense a subject is relevant if it deals with current happenings. Thus a Greek tragedy or the history of the United States would not be relevant, whereas productions by avant-garde dramatists or racial conflicts in America today would be. But to use the word "relevant" in this way confuses what is topical with what is timely. The plays of Sophocles were topical only during the golden age of Athens, but they are timely in every age, for they never lose their power to enrich personal experience and deepen our response to the human condition. Slaves in America were freed by 1865, but an understanding of their lives prior to then provides important insights into current social tensions. To confine a liberal education to what is topical would exclude much material of value to all members of a democracy, and so, given that meaning of the term, a liberal education need not be relevant.

On occasion, however, "relevant" is used to refer to any subject concerned with the nature, origin, or solution of the fundamental social, political, intellectual, or moral problems of our time. In this sense a liberal education is indeed relevant, since its very purpose is to enable citizens to make wise decisions about the issues confronting them.

But to avoid distorting this notion of relevance, certain precautions are in order. Not every problem is a fundamental one. A liberal education should, for example, shed light on the nature of capitalism, not merely devise plans to increase sales in a local store. Whatever the heuristic value of such case studies, intellectual perspective involves the power of abstraction.

It must also be emphasized that certain knowledge and skills not explicitly related to any specific contemporary problems are nevertheless crucial to a liberal education, since they form the basis for an intelligent approach to all problems. As we have seen, without linguistic and mathematical facility, without the power of critical thinking, without philosophical sophistication, it would be impossible to deal adequately with the crises of the age.

In addition, concentration upon contemporary events may result in a failure to recognize how inextricably they are tied to the past and how much can be learned about them through a study of the past. The urgencies of present problems should not mislead us into overlooking their historical background, for in order to know where you are going, it is advantageous to know where you have been.

One final note. I have described the content of a liberal education without providing particulars, for they necessarily vary within a changing world. We face difficulties unknown to our ancestors and likely to be forgotten by our descendants. The strength of a liberal education lies in its adaptability to each generation's problems, whether they be long-standing or of recent vintage. What we need to learn depends upon what we need to do, and while some needs remain constant, others are mutable. How easy it is to forget that the intellectual giants who contributed to the making of the modern mind were themselves breakers of tradition, impelled to forge new tools in an effort to handle what were for them the issues of the day.

Chapter 3

Schools

The very title of this chapter is apt to depress certain readers. Learning, they would say, is admirable, but must we have the tedium of classrooms, courses, and credits? Cannot education proceed without schools?

Unquestionably some individuals have attained intellectual sophistication without much formal instruction. But such cases, even when vividly presented, do not constitute a strong argument against colleges. The test of the effectiveness of a social policy, whether it be fire protection, highway construction, or medicare, is not whether all individuals require it, but whether a significant number do. Remember democracy's commitment to provide a liberal education for as many citizens as possible. It seems plausible to suggest that the most effective means of achieving this goal is the establishment of publicly recognized institutions explicitly designed, staffed, and equipped to afford large numbers of people the higher learning they need.

Things are not quite so simple, however, for we must consider carefully a frequently stated challenge to the belief that classrooms provide the appropriate environment for obtaining a worthwhile education. How often someone remarks that the most valuable sort of learning occurs outside, not inside, the classroom, that the way to acquire significant knowledge is to take a job, travel, or simply interact with others, since life itself furnishes the best education. And this view has many times been supported by the observation that even the most brilliant college graduate may exhibit extraordinary naïveté or insensitivity when he endeavors to make his way in the world.

This skepticism regarding the value of schooling demands a detailed reply, since it rests upon a healthy dose of common sense conjoined with several basic misunderstandings. To begin with, we should recognize that character is not developed primarily in a classroom setting. A school cannot be expected to instill decent behavior in those whose moral education has been disregarded or mangled by family and community. Nor is practical wisdom a product of college courses. Its source is, I think, unknown; we may suppose it partly a result of habit, partly a result of informal teaching, and perhaps partly, as the ancient Greeks would have said, a gift of the gods. Individuals with college degrees are no more virtuous or prudent than anyone else; supposing otherwise attributes to a liberal education wondrous qualities it does not possess.

A classroom, although not the gateway to happiness, does provide the opportunity to step back from the pressures of the moment and examine with expert guidance important bodies of knowledge, sophisticated techniques of analysis, and profound works of the imagination, all affording increased awareness and understanding of the world's complexities. Field study can also be valuable, but if it is to contribute to a student's liberal education, it must be structured for that purpose, and some reasonable means should be employed to determine what has been learned.

For instance, contrary to a common misconception, working in an election campaign is not equivalent to a systematic study of the American political system, just as sexual activity is not equivalent to a systematic study of human sexuality. Insight into fundamental problems is not gained simply by immersion in the stream of experience; indeed, the rush of events may evoke unthinking responses and encourage the development of weak qualities of mind that hinder learning rather than fostering it.

A resident of a metropolis with a high crime rate is likely to be aware of that problem but may believe it to be explainable in terms of some outlandish theory of racial inferiority rather than recognizing, as any competent social scientist would, its connection to poverty or drug addiction. In other words, living with a difficulty does not guarantee an informed approach to its solution. Indeed, the key to grasping the essential elements of a situation is not necessarily to be found in prolonged firsthand exposure to it. The single most impressive sociological study of American democratic life was the work of Alexis de Tocqueville, a young Frenchman who visited these shores for less than a year.[1]

Experience is the source of education, but not all

experiences are equally educative. A school environment is expressly designed to maximize opportunities for learning, and so, not surprisingly, the
most reliable method of obtaining a liberal education
is to attend a school offering such a course of study.

The advantages of formal schooling are clear. At
hand are laboratories, a library, and other aids to
learning. Faculty members, selected on the basis of
their expertise, plan the curriculum seeking to insti-
tute as balanced and comprehensive a set of offerings
as possible. The presence of other students stimulates
discussion and affords the opportunity to hear advo-
cates of differing points of view. Administrators
smooth day-to-day operations while defending the
entire enterprise against those who knowingly or
unknowingly would undermine its ideals.

All these factors may seem too obvious to mention, but even truisms need emphasis when they are
forgotten. Since those who support the value of a
college education so often find themselves on the de-
fensive trying to account for the supposed inefficien-
cies or inadequacies of their institutions, we must
remind ourselves that not only is there a case to be
made against schools, there is also a case to be made
for them.

No matter how strong a person's dedication to
learning, the barriers to self-education are formidable without the groundwork provided by formal instruction. Anyone may informally acquire hobbies
such as stamp-collecting, gardening, or bridge, but
when did you last meet someone who without
academic background was pursuing on his own the
study of quantum mechanics, macroeconomic theory,
or epistemology? An individual may with the best of
intentions obtain books dealing with these subjects,
but after reading only a few pages he is apt to become

discouraged, for the complexities render substantial progress virtually hopeless without the encouragement and direction provided by a teacher within an environment structured for learning. Reading lists, course outlines, lectures, discussion sections, and laboratory periods are not impediments but aids to education. Without them, we would normally be overwhelmed by the difficulties inherent in mastering formidable material.

Another advantage to college study is that although particular instructors may prove disappointing, at least we are assured that all faculty members were chosen by their peers. Suppose whenever we wished to study a subject, it was our responsibility to find an appropriate teacher. Not having a grasp of the field, how could we reliably distinguish the expert from the charlatan? Chaos would ensue.

Those who are suspicious of the authority of faculties have occasionally proposed that schools should operate like libraries. Anyone may receive a library card, borrow the books of his choice, read them or not as he pleases, and return them with no questions asked. If a school were to function similarly, anyone could be admitted, attend whichever courses he wished, do whatever work he liked, and leave without being tested. Professors would thus be viewed as educational resources rather than arbiters of standards.

Some universities conduct their extension divisions partly along these lines, but carried to an extreme, this proposal would destroy the concept of a college degree. No one is honored for having made extensive use of a library, nor are librarians expected to certify book borrowers as learned readers. But a democratic society, wishing to emphasize the importance of a liberal education, requires some means of public recognition for those who have achieved it. An appropriate degree serves that purpose. And its worth rests on the expertise of the faculty who award it. Thus, although a library is crucial to the intellectual life of a college, a school is not merely a library and professors are not just animated reference works. On the contrary, they are the guardians of the worth of the college diploma which symbolizes democracy's commitment to liberal education.

However, even with all the words of praise we can muster in behalf of schools, it must be admitted that far too many people look back on experiences there as tedious, onerous, even dispiriting. If schools are dedicated to such high ideals, if they are crucial to the welfare of a democratic society, why do they so often generate unhappiness?

In later chapters I shall identify and suggest remedies for the most important causes of student distress, but, sad to say, not all the discomfort is entirely avoidable. This outlook may seem unduly pessimistic, but since most of us realize that the goods of this world have their cost, we should not be surprised to find this principle at work in the educational sphere. A good teacher can alleviate the pains of learning, but not even a great teacher can eradicate them. Despite what the best-intentioned of reformers may promise, not all education can be turned into sheer ecstasy.

Chapter 4

The Myth of the Royal Road

Euclid, the Greek mathematician, was once asked whether there was a simple way to comprehend his monumental treatise, the *Elements*. He replied, "There is no royal road to geometry." That insight is equally applicable to every field of serious endeavor. Whether one sets out to become skilled at cooking, golf, violin-playing, or chemistry, there is no easy path to mastery.

However, students have often been led to believe that they can achieve without effort, that to obtain a good education they need only skip blithely down the royal road to learning. Unfortunately, that way is no more than a detour to the dead end of ignorance.

Becoming an educated person is a difficult, demanding enterprise. Just as anyone who spoke of intense physical training as a continuous source of pleasure and delight would be thought a fool, for we all know how much pain and frustration such training involves, so anyone who speaks of intense mental exertion as a continuous source of joy and ecstasy ought to be thought equally foolish, for such effort also involves pain and frustration. It is painful to have one's ignorance exposed and frustrating to be baffled by intellectual subtleties. Of course, there can be joy in learning as there can be joy in sport. But in both cases the joy is a result of overcoming genuine challenges and cannot be experienced without toil.

It is not easy to read intelligently and think precisely. It is not easy to speak fluently and write clearly. It is not easy to study a subject carefully and know it thoroughly. But these abilities are the foundation of a sound liberal education. As Jacques Barzun has observed, "Of what use to even an unusually bright pupil are all the visual aids, paperback books, field trips, documentary movies, special lectures, and 'opportunities for independent work' if he lacks the categories of thought and habits of study which would enable his impressions to cohere?"[1]

Although every member of a democracy is equally entitled to express his opinions, not all expressed opinions are equally sound. Some arguments are valid, some invalid. Some hypotheses are well-founded, some not. A claim may be self-contradictory, it may run counter to the available evidence, its meaning may be unclear, or it may mean nothing at all. An educated person does not simply believe; he believes what he can explain and cogently defend.

Students must learn that not every piece of work is good work. In fact, some work is just no good at all. An individual may be friendly, cooperative, and sensitive to the needs of mankind, but he may nevertheless produce a muddled economics paper or an incompetent laboratory report. And that he means well is no justification for an inadequate performance. Good intentions do not obliterate the difference between clarity and obscurity, accuracy and carelessness, knowledge and ignorance.

A desire to learn is not by itself equivalent to learning. Having ambitions is easy; what is difficult is fulfilling them. So many of us go through life aware of our aptitudes and abilities but never developing them. We are left consoling ourselves with the thought, "I could have if only . . ."

One example of such wasted gifts often comes to my mind. Many years ago I attended a summer camp that emphasized sports. Among the many good athletes there, one in particular stood out. He was only fifteen, but his prowess was remarkable, and since baseball was the game he loved, everyone assumed he would one day be a major-league star.

I heard nothing further about him until years later, when at a reunion I saw him participating in an old-timer's game. Although still outstanding, he was overweight and considerably slower than in his camp days. Later he told me he had played briefly in the minor leagues but had soon given up baseball and become a construction worker. His voice was quiet, as of one whose dream had long since faded.

When I asked a veteran counselor who had known him all his life how such a superb athlete could have failed, this was the response: "Sure he loved to play baseball, but that's all he would do— play it. He wasn't willing to work at it. Fielding ground balls at training camp may be fun for a while, but as the hours pass the fun disappears. The strain begins to tell and the field empties. Before long just a few men are still practicing. They're the only ones with a real chance to make the majors. The rest better find something else to do."

The ability to work, aptly termed "self-discipline," was felicitously described by John Dewey as "power at command . . . a power to endure in an intelligently chosen course in face of distraction, confusion, and difficulty. . . ."[2] It is a prime requisite for the achievement of worthwhile goals, for, as noted previously, the road to mastering any significant skill is not an easy one. Distractions, confusions, and difficulties abound. Only the individual who persists in the face of such obstacles can succeed, and talent is insufficient where self-discipline is lacking.

Thus, one reason for the negative image of schools is now apparent. In a classroom students face not only the adventures of learning but also the hardships. Grasping a subject requires mastery of its complexities, and, in attempting to gain understanding, a person is apt to lose his way, become discouraged, and grow impatient. To suggest that such problems are entirely avoidable is pedagogic pap.

Acquiring an education involves not mere flights of fancy but careful study, a concern for detail, and the fortitude to carry projects through to completion regardless of their appeal. Even the enrichment of the imagination demands intense concentration. Teaching music, for example, does not consist of playing records for a student and awaiting his haphazard responses. He must learn the structure of a fugue, the difference between tonality and atonality, and how a theme is treated in a set of variations. There is, of course, more to music than knowing the difference between a symphony and a concerto, but without such essentials the rest is bluff and fluff.

Although dwelling on the sweat and tears of learning may become disheartening, awareness of these difficulties affords the opportunity for dealing with them effectively. And devising methods of doing so is a crucial component of good teaching.

Chapter 5

The Art of Instruction

A teacher is responsible both to his students and his subject. Sacrificing either one for the other amounts to failure.

Consider the simple case of teaching a friend how to play chess. You begin by explaining the different possible moves of the various pieces, and soon your friend assures you he has grasped these basic maneuvers. Suppose then, after stressing the importance of strong openings, you proceed to demonstrate your favorite, the slashing King's Gambit. Knights, bishops, and pawns whiz back and forth over the board, accompanied by your running commentary on the strengths and weaknesses of such variations as the Cunningham Gambit, the Kieseritzky Gambit, and the ever-dangerous Falkbeer Counter Gambit.

At last, you complete this detailed analysis and look up proudly, awaiting your friend's approval. He stares at the board, shakes his head, and finally remarks, "I guess I'll stick to checkers. I like it better when all the pieces move the same way."

What is the problem? Your presentation of the King's Gambit may have been flawless, but while concentrating on the details of the subvariations, you have overlooked your friend's confusion as he tried to keep in mind such fundamentals as how pawns may move and where knights may jump. A good instructor anticipates such difficulties, realizing how tenuous a beginning student's claim to understanding can be. Lacking this insight, you may be succeeding as a chess analyst, but not as a chess teacher.

Assume, however, that in an effort to sustain your friend's involvement, you do not warn him about the complexities of opening theory, but merely advise that he attack quickly with his queen. You regale him with anecdotes of your triumphs over weak players who fell into such elementary traps as the Fool's Mate. Your friend supposes he has mastered a surefire strategy and, full of confidence and enthusiasm, marches to the nearest chess club. There he soon encounters some intermediate players who deftly parry his premature assaults and laughingly defeat him with ease.

What went wrong this time? Unless your friend eventually realizes the inadequacy of the preparation you provided and possesses the dedication to study the technical materials you suggested he bypass, he will again and again be beaten badly, quickly grow discouraged, and perhaps give up the game altogether. He may, nevertheless, have thoroughly enjoyed his lessons with you. If so, you succeeded as an entertainer, but again not as a teacher.

Anyone who thinks teaching is easy has never stood in front of a class of thirty, restless teenagers and tried to arouse and maintain their interest while simultaneously attempting to communicate a subject's complexities. In such circumstances a person quickly becomes aware that not everyone cares who he is or what he has to say.

Of course, the mechanics of sheer drill backed by the pressures of reward and punishment will normally result in some learning. But if a student's attention is engaged only by gold stars or raps on the knuckles, the removal of these reinforcements may well be accompanied by loss of interest. He will thus have failed to acquire that most important of qualities, the desire to continue learning. An individual whose education ends when he leaves school is doomed to spend much of his life in ignorance. Good teaching, therefore, is not merely the transmission of information and skills, but the encouragement of zest for further study.

Sheer gusto, however, is not sufficient. If it were, a teacher could succeed merely by going along with the whims of his students. If they wanted to learn history but not economics, he could teach history and not economics. If they found most history boring but were fascinated by the history of the American cowboy, he could teach that history and nothing else. If they wanted to see cowboy movies but not read any books about the West, he could turn his classroom into a movie house. And if they wanted just to picnic in the park, he could make himself useful cooking the hamburgers.

But since we have already recognized the critical role played by formal education in preserving and enriching a democratic society, it follows that student vagaries cannot be allowed to dictate educational

policy. A student's interests may well not coincide
with his needs. A teacher, therefore, has the responsibility to lead his students to master appropriate
subject matter without misrepresenting or diluting
it, yet at the same time arousing appreciation for it.
How can he achieve this result?

Since teaching is a creative endeavor, there are
no infallible guides to success. Good instruction,
however, typically involves four elements: motivation, organization, clarification, and generalization.
Let us consider each in turn.

As to motivation, I have found it useful to distinguish two types of teachers: one pulls the subject
matter behind him, the other pushes the subject matter in front of him. The former uses his own personality to attract students and then tries to transfer
the students' interest from himself to his subject. The
latter minimizes his own personality and seeks to
interest students directly in the material itself.

One who pulls the subject behind him usually
has little difficulty in arousing enthusiasm, but his
characteristic pitfall is the failure to redirect student
interest away from himself and toward his subject
matter. He may become a friend of the students, yet
fail to teach them anything. As Sidney Hook has
perceptively remarked, a teacher " . . . must be
friendly without becoming a friend, although he may
pave the way for later friendship, for friendship is a
mark of preference and expresses itself in indulgence,
favors, and distinctions that unconsciously find an
invidious form. . . . A teacher who becomes 'just one
of the boys,' who courts popularity, who builds up
personal loyalty in exchange for indulgent treatment, has missed his vocation. He should leave the
classroom for professional politics."[1]

But this is not to say that a teacher who pulls the

subject behind him cannot be a superb instructor. Indeed, if he succeeds in involving students as much in the material as in his own manner, he can exert an enormously beneficial influence on an extraordinary number, for such a teacher invariably attracts many devoted admirers who will follow wherever he leads, even down the rugged road of learning.

On the other hand, one who pushes the subject in front of him need have no worry about misdirecting a student's interest; his worry is whether such interest will be aroused at all. In many cases he must overcome the necessarily abstract quality of his subject and make apparent the connections between the seemingly esoteric material and his students' own sphere of experience. Perhaps the most reliable tool for doing so, and one he certainly must master, is the use of well-chosen examples that relate to the purposes or passions of the students. The subject itself thus becomes their personal concern.

But whatever the particular approach of his instructor, a student will hopefully be led to appreciate the subject not merely as a means but as an end, something of intrinsic worth to be enjoyed on its own account. His life will thereby be enriched and the material rendered more vivid and even more useful when serving some purpose beyond itself.

A teacher who fails to convey the significance of what he is discussing can see his own inadequacy reflected in the eyes of his apathetic students. Obtaining a sound liberal education is difficult enough for a person interested in his work; for one who is bored the process is intolerable.

A motivated student is ready to learn, but a teacher must be organized enough to take advantage of this situation. Admittedly, inflexibility can hinder an instructor from making the most of opportunities that arise spontaneously in the course of discussion, but a rambling presentation may well dissipate initial enthusiasm. What is too often forgotten is that lack of planning usually leads to stream-of-consciousness instruction, resulting in the sort of class that meanders idly from one topic to another, amounting to nothing more than an hour of aimless talk.

Each day before he sets foot in the classroom, a teacher should decide exactly what he intends to accomplish during that particular session and precisely what he expects his students to know by the time the period ends. In Whitehead's words, "a certain ruthless definiteness is essential in education." [2] A teacher's obligation is to guide students, and to guide requires a sense of where one is headed. If the teacher himself does not know, then everyone is lost.

Careful organization, however, must be complemented by an equal concern for clarification. Otherwise, even the most highly structured course of study may prove incomprehensible to the uninitiated.

Since academic subjects tend toward complexity, classrooms are often rife with confusion. But a good teacher foresees this problem and substantially reduces it by making every effort to be as clear as possible. He uses concrete cases to exemplify abstract concepts, and, realizing that individuals differ in how they arrive at an understanding of particular ideas, he takes pains to explain fundamental principles in a variety of ways.

Of course, not every train of thought can be rendered in very simple terms. A book entitled *Kant Made Easy* is surely the work of a charlatan or a fool. An effective teacher, therefore, must be a shrewd judge of both the difficulty of his material and the ability of his students.

Why do some instructors seem to make so little effort to express themselves clearly? Many do not realize that a good teacher directs his remarks not only at the best student, or at the top ten percent of the class, or even at the majority; instead, he speaks so that virtually all his listeners can follow. He realizes that when more than one or two students complain they are lost, many others, whether they themselves realize it or not, are also in need of help.

Unfortunately, it must be admitted that a few teachers are not interested in clarifying matters. They mistake obscurity for profundity. One supposes that their idea of a good time would be delivering a speech in Turkish to an audience that only understood English. How a school can protect itself against such pedagogic insensitivity will be considered later.

Having now discussed motivation, organization, and clarification, we turn to the fourth element of good instruction: generalization. Because a thorough knowledge of any subject matter depends upon a firm grasp of its details, the tendency of many instructors is to emphasize analysis at the expense of synthesis. But to master a subject requires awareness of its overall structure and a sense of its connection to related areas of inquiry. Details are necessary to understanding, but they are not sufficient. Also required is perspective, and that can be achieved only by viewing individual facts within a broad framework.

I still vividly recall my high school history teacher who insisted that we memorize the dates, locations, and names of the commanding generals for every major battle of the Civil War. Only in my college years when I heard a series of enthralling lectures on the causes, strategies, and results of that war did I come to understand and share my earlier teacher's fascination with the events of that period.[3]

A student should not be allowed to become lost in minutiae. For although generalizations without details are hollow, details without generalizations are barren.

We have thus far been considering the components of good teaching, but great teaching involves yet an additional element. The great teacher not only motivates his students, organizes the class, clarifies his material, and provides illuminating generalizations; in addition, he projects a vision of excellence. And this central notion deserves special consideration.

Chapter 6

Excellence

The mere mention of excellence delights some people and distresses others. However, these different reactions stem not necessarily from any fundamental disagreement but perhaps from an ambiguity lurking in the concept itself.

In one sense excellence is equivalent to superiority. Given this definition, one achieves excellence by surpassing others, however strong or weak the opposition may be. Thus, each valedictorian, ranking first among his classmates in scholarship, is by definition an excellent student.

But in another sense excellence is equivalent to merit. According to this usage, an individual is excellent if he is worthy of high commendation, regardless of how many others deserve similar praise. For example, we speak of being in excellent health, possessing an excellent moral character, or compiling an excellent attendance record. Note that many of us are in excellent health, not just a few. And numerous persons are of excellent moral character, for one individual's noble action does not preclude another's; indeed, it may encourage it. Likewise, all students may have excellent attendance records, since the presence of one does not require the absence of others.

Excellence as merit implies a competition against standards; many can win, many can lose. Excellence as superiority implies a competition against others; few can win, most must lose.

Superiority, however, is not necessarily praiseworthy. Consider students who have just been graduated from a very poor medical school. Even the best of them may not be an effective physician. Superiority is a laudable goal only if accompanied by merit, for to surpass others is a dubious achievement when none is of high quality. Thus, the ideal of excellence should be understood as referring to merit, not superiority.

But those who denigrate excellence usually equate it with superiority. And their opposition is based on an antipathy to the ruthlessness that is too often a part of competition. But if in opposing the excesses of bitter rivalry we fail to recognize the difference between what is of high quality and what is not, the result is confusion.

Consider, for instance, a passage from Charles A. Reich's much-discussed book, *The Greening of America*. After claiming that the younger generation "rejects the whole concept of excellence and comparative merit," he offers the following defense of its viewpoint. "Each person has his own individuality, not to be compared to that of anyone else. Someone may be a brilliant thinker, but he is not 'better' at thinking than anyone else, he simply possesses his own excellence. A person who thinks very poorly is still excellent in his own way."[1]

Reich is here so concerned about avoiding inter-personal comparisons that his position collapses into incoherence. If one individual is a brilliant thinker and another thinks very poorly, then to avoid contradiction it must be admitted that the first is better at thinking than the second. Furthermore, the first is a thinker of merit, whereas the second, whatever his other virtues, is not. And despite Reich's optimism, the second may not possess any notable virtues. In that case he would not be "excellent in his own way"; he would not be excellent in any way.

To insist upon such truisms is not to deny individuality, for that notion rests upon differences among people. If you are skilled at golf but inept at gardening, while your neighbor can plant but not putt, why pretend that each of you is proficient at both activities? Surely individuality can be preserved without resorting to the obvious fiction that everyone is excellent at everything.

Sensible judgments of merit depend upon reasonable standards, and these must be established on the basis of knowledge and experience. How, for example, can we judiciously decide whether an individual is an excellent beekeeper, if we are ignorant regarding apiculture and the skills of those who have practiced it? With such information in hand, however, appropriate criteria of merit become apparent and may be met by many or by few.

At this point it should be emphasized that, contrary to a common misconception, value judgments are not merely statements of conscience or expressions of individual preference. Most, perhaps all, of them can be rationally discussed and are open to confirmation or refutation.

Suppose, for instance, you are a member of an organization that participates in a softball league. You are told by your friend Ferguson that a fellow named Benson is an excellent ballplayer. You ask Benson to join your team, and he is happy to do so. But he turns out to be woefully inadequate. He drops balls thrown to him, lets ground balls through his legs, and strikes out almost every time he comes to bat. You tell Ferguson that his recommendation of Benson was a mistake. Either Ferguson does not know what a good ballplayer is or someone has misled him about Benson's capabilities, for obviously Benson is not a good player.

Notice that when you say Benson is not a good player, there is nothing necessarily emotional or unclear about your statement. You are not just expressing your preference, nor are you appealing to the dictates of your conscience. To say Benson is not a good ballplayer is to say that he hits poorly and fields inadequately. To defend your view all you need do is point to his batting and fielding averages. Although there may be some disagreement as to whether a player who bats .250 and commits a number of errors is a good player, there is no doubt whatever that an individual who bats .200 and commits errors in every game is not a good player, while an individual who bats .300 and hardly ever commits an error is a good player. In other words, the distinction between good and bad players is a clear one, despite the possibility of borderline cases, just as the distinction between bald and hirsute men is a clear one, despite the possibility of borderline cases.

Note also that it would be senseless to say that although Benson hits and fields well, he still lacks one attribute of an all-star, namely, goodness, because if Benson could hit and field well, he would be a good softball player. Goodness is not another attribute beside these abilities; it is simply a shorthand way of referring to them.

Suppose when you tell Ferguson that Benson is not a good player, Ferguson replies that you are mistaken, for he has seen Benson play in practice and there he hits balls over the fence and fields flawlessly. How would you reply to Ferguson? You would not say that since value judgments are just matters of preference, there is no reasonable method of deciding whether Benson is a good player. Nor would you appeal to Ferguson's conscience in an effort to persuade him of your point of view. All you need do to convince him he is mistaken is to explain that sometimes an individual performs well in practice but plays badly in league games. To defend your claim, you might simply point out that in the first twenty games of the season, Benson batted .075 and committed thirty-one errors. Ferguson would no doubt be amazed at these statistics but would surely agree that although Benson is impressive in practice, he is at present not a good player under game conditions. Here then we have a clear example of a disagreement about values that has been resolved by an appeal to the facts.

Of course, not all cases can be handled so neatly, and a great deal more might be said about the role reason can play in the resolution of such disagreements.[2] But complicated variations should not obscure the basic theme: appropriate criteria of merit can be determined rationally. To do so we need to recognize that good pilots, good physicists, and good pediatricians are good for different reasons, and that these reasons depend upon the specific aims of the various pursuits. That is why intelligent evaluation of performance is impossible without detailed understanding of the activity in question.

In the previous chapter I described a great teacher as projecting a vision of excellence, and now that view can be developed. A beginning student, due to unfamiliarity with the field he is studying, is apt to have little sense of the difference between acceptable and unacceptable work. That is why a novice chess player can be impressed by the supposed profundity of superficial combinations. But such naïveté soon vanishes, for how much sophistication is needed to differentiate a weak tennis player from a sound one, or a poor pianist from an able performer?

What is not so easy to distinguish, even after study, is the difference between what is adequate and what is excellent. How many of us, observing two physicians, would know which was merely competent and which superb? How many of us, reading a history of Europe, would realize whether the account was exceptional or just satisfactory? Recognizing such distinctions depends upon an awareness of critical subtleties, and each great teacher in his own distinctive ways leads his students to acquire and prize such insight.

Those who attain excellence know the sense of satisfaction that accompanies such success. But excellence is not only of value to those who possess it. Equally important is its significance for those who learn to appreciate it, for by developing the acuity and sensitivity needed to comprehend the magnificent achievements of which human effort is capable, one's perceptions are rendered more vivid and one's experience enormously enriched.

The Declaration of Independence proclaims that "all men are created equal," thus reminding us that in a democracy all persons possess equal rights and deserve equal consideration. But nowhere does that document state or imply that all people are equal in their creations. Although the well-being of a democratic society does not rest upon any of us matching the extraordinary accomplishments of Benjamin Franklin or Thomas Jefferson, it does depend upon our recognizing quality, respecting quality, and rewarding quality, for excellence must be nurtured if it is to thrive. That is why, in Jacques Barzun's words, "we shall never have excellence unless we are willing to distinguish it in public from mediocrity."[3]

If the ideal of excellence is to play a central role in the educational process, those who are knowledgeable in a particular field must be willing to judge fairly the efforts of those who are attempting to acquire mastery. Yet no issues are more controversial than those surrounding the most commonly used instruments of evaluation: examinations and grades. The very idea of employing these tools is anathema to many people, and the serious doubts they raise deserve extended discussion.

Chapter 7

The Case for Examinations and Grades

It is astonishing to realize how little a college teacher may know about the academic lives of his students, and conversely, how little his students may know about the academic life of their teacher. I recall one professor who taught a large lecture course for several years without ever realizing he was addressing a captive audience, since, unbeknownst to him, the course was required for graduation. On the other hand, I have spoken to students unaware that just as a student can be required to take a course he would prefer not to take, so a teacher can be required to teach a course he would prefer not to teach. How many teachers, even in a very small class, know whether their students are sophomores or seniors, a matter of some importance to the students? But again, how many students know whether their teacher is an assistant or full professor, a matter of some importance to the teacher? It may never occur to a teacher that the sleepy students in his 8:00 A.M. class are there only because all other sections of the course were already closed when they registered. But, likewise, it may never occur to the students in the 8:00 A.M. class that their teacher is standing wearily before them at such an hour only because he lacks the seniority to claim any other time.

Such mutual ignorance extends over many aspects of academic life and is nowhere more apparent than in matters regarding examinations and grades. A basic source of the misunderstandings which surround evaluations of student work lies in the fact that normally such evaluation has vital consequences for the one being evaluated, whereas it has no such consequences for the one who does the evaluating. The grades a student receives not only determine whether he graduates with honors or fails out of school; they may also guide him in choosing his field of specialization, affect his plans for graduate study, and ultimately influence his choice of career. On the other hand, the grades a teacher gives do not affect his professional stature, his commitment to a field of study, or his future success as a scholar. A student may for a long time harbor a deep resentment against a teacher who grades him harshly, but were he to confront that teacher years later, the teacher might not even remember the student and would almost surely not remember the grade. Indeed, the teacher would most probably be astounded to learn the student cared so deeply about the grade. I once heard a woman who had taught for over thirty years remark in a faculty meeting that she could not understand why students were so interested in grades. Apparently in moving from one side of the desk to the other she had developed amnesia.

Some students believe that teachers are fond of examinations and grades, that they employ these devices in order to retain power over students. But although undoubtedly a few teachers do possess such motives, most do not. A scholar enjoys reading and writing books, not making up questions to test the knowledge others may possess. And one can find a great many more fascinating things to do than read one hundred or so answers to the same question and try to decide how many points each answer is worth. Whether Johnny understands the problem of induction is not crucial to Professor Smith's intellectual life, for Professor Smith finds the problem highly stimulating, even if Johnny neglects to study it.

The system of examinations and grades thus places important decisions affecting students' lives in the hands of those who are comparatively unaffected by these decisions and perhaps quite uninterested in making them. Such a situation is fraught with unpleasant possibilities, these often compounded by the difficulty of constructing and applying suitable examination and grading procedures. But to refer to "suitable examination and grading procedures" implies that such procedures are intended to fulfill certain worthwhile aims, and so we would do well to consider just what those aims are. In other words, why bother with examinations or grades at all?

Examinations ideally serve at least four significant purposes. First, an examination provides the opportunity for a student to discover the scope and depth of his knowledge. Much like an athlete who tests himself under game conditions or like a violinist who tests himself under concert conditions, a student tests himself under examination conditions and

thereby determines whether he is in complete control
of certain material or whether he possesses merely a
tenuous grasp of it. It is one thing to speak glibly
about a subject; it is something else to answer specific
questions about that subject, relying solely upon
one's own knowledge and committing answers to
paper so they can be scrutinized by experts in the
field. A proper examination procedure makes clear to
the student what he knows and what he does not
know and thus can serve as a valuable guide to
further study. By paying close attention to the results
of his examination, a student can become aware of his
strengths and weaknesses. He can learn whether his
methods of study are effective, and he can recognize
the areas of a subject in which he needs to concentrate
his future efforts. In short, an examination enables a
student to find out how well he is doing and assists
him in deciding how he can do better.

Students, however, are not the only ones who are
tested by an examination, for the second purpose
examinations should serve is to provide an opportunity for a teacher to discover how effective his teaching has been. By carefully analyzing his students'
examination papers, a teacher can learn in what
ways he has succeeded and in what ways he has
failed. Many instructors would prefer to believe the
reason three-quarters of their students missed a particular question is that the students are not bright or
have not studied hard enough. But in this matter
college teachers have something to learn from those
who teach in elementary school. When three-
quarters of an ordinary third-grade class find multi-
plication confusing, the teacher does not assume the
students are not bright or have not studied hard
enough. He assumes his teaching methods are in
need of improvement. A college teacher ought to ar-

rive at the same conclusion when three-quarters of his class are confused by a fundamental point he thought he had explained clearly. In one sense, then, teachers as well as students can pass or fail examinations, for by paying close attention to the results of his students' efforts, a teacher can become aware of the strengths and weaknesses of his instruction. He can learn whether his methods are effective, and he can recognize the areas of a subject in which he needs to concentrate his future efforts. In short, an examination enables a teacher to find out how well he is doing and assists him in deciding how he can do better.

We have thus far considered examinations only as tests of learning, but they can be more than a means of evaluating previous learning experiences; they can be themselves worthwhile learning experiences. During an examination most students are working with an extraordinarily high degree of concentration. If the examination questions place familiar material in a slightly unfamiliar light and thereby lead students to develop for themselves significant connections between various aspects of the subject matter, then the students will be working intensely on challenging, important problems and so gain intellectual perspective. Ironically, in this day of large lecture classes, examinations sometimes provide greater opportunity for active learning than any other part of the course. It is not unusual to hear student complaints about uninspired, unrewarding examinations. Such complaints are entirely legitimate, for a boring, banal examination indicates pedagogic laziness and is a waste of a potentially valuable learning experience. Long after completing a course, students who have forgotten virtually everything else may still remember some of the

examination questions. They should be worth re-
membering.

An examination, however, consists of more than
the two or three hours spent sitting in the examination room. Most students prepare for examinations,
and such preparation itself possesses significant educational value. The nature of an examination requires that one not know what questions will be
asked or which aspects of the subject matter spot-
lighted. The only adequate preparation for an examination is a thorough study of all the subject matter
and a careful consideration of as many as possible of
its various interconnections. In trying to anticipate
the examination questions, a student is led to analyze and synthesize the course material, thereby
strengthening and solidifying his grasp of the subject
matter.

In this connection it is important to note that the
writing of a term paper, though potentially a beneficial educational experience, is not a suitable substitute for preparing for an examination. In writing a
term paper, even one which is given a strict time limit
and misleadingly dubbed a "take-home examination,"
a student needs only to master those parts of the
course material bearing directly on his topic. Rarely
does a term paper require mastery of most or even
very much of the course material. Furthermore, it is
not difficult to copy ideas from a book, alter them
slightly so as to avoid the charge of plagiarism, and
use them in a term paper without ever thoroughly
understanding them. Such a tactic is almost impossible in an examination, for few students have a strong
enough memory to answer questions intelligently
without understanding their answers. Thus, preparing for an examination is in some ways, though not
all, more demanding and more rewarding than writing a term paper.

This fact was strikingly brought to my attention several years ago by a student who came to see me after I had returned her examination paper. She had received a C and was very disappointed, for, as she explained, she had always been an A student. I asked her whether she had studied as hard for this examination as for previous ones, and to my surprise she informed me that never before in her academic career had she taken an examination. As it turned out, she had gone to a secondary school where examinations were considered outmoded, and had then for two years attended a college that prided itself on having replaced all examinations with term papers. I was fascinated by this woman's academic background and inquired whether she thought she had been helped or hindered by it. She replied that until she had taken this examination she had always assumed it was to her advantage to have avoided the pressure of examinations, but that now she believed her grasp of previous course material rather flimsy. She had learned how to write term papers but never had thoroughly mastered an entire body of material so that she could draw upon it at will and utilize it effectively wherever it was called for. In short, she had never received the benefits of preparing for an examination.

Of course, examinations serve yet another purpose, for they are in part the basis on which course grades are determined. However, since we have already seen that examinations provide an opportunity to discover the scope and depth of a student's knowledge, we have little reason to doubt that if grades are to be given, they should be based, at least to some extent, on the results of examinations. The crucial question is: Why should grades be given?

Ideally, a grade represents an expert's opinion of the quality of a student's work within a specified area of inquiry. Viewed in this perspective, a grade serves a variety of significant educational purposes. First, it is to a student's advantage to be aware of his level of achievement, for that information can be a valuable aid to him in assessing his past efforts, evaluating his present abilities, and formulating his future plans. Knowing whether one's approach to a subject has been fruitful is a helpful guide toward further study; recognizing one's strengths and weaknesses is vital to intellectual growth as well as to decisions regarding how one's abilities might most effectively be utilized in and out of school. A college student is directly concerned with questions such as: Which courses should I take? Which fields should I specialize in? Which graduate schools, if any, should I apply to? Which career should I choose? Intelligent answers to all these questions depend, among other factors, upon the individual's academic abilities and accomplishments, and he can measure these reliably, though not infallibly, by his grades. Granted a teacher's judgment may occasionally be mistaken, at least it is based upon relevant expertise and experience and is not subject to the sort of delusions which so often distort self-evaluation. A student may not always be pleased by the knowledge grades afford, but the important point is that such knowledge is almost always useful to him.

Students, though, are not the only ones to whom such knowledge is useful, for in order for a teacher to provide the detailed educational advice often so helpful to a student, he needs to have an exact record of the student's academic performance. How can a teacher intelligently advise a student in choosing his program of study and in planning for the years after graduation if an accurate measure of the student's level of achievement is unavailable? If, for example, a chemistry teacher does not know how well a student has done in his various science and mathematics courses, how can the teacher intelligently advise the student which level of chemistry to study, which areas in the student's background need strengthening, and whether it is reasonable for the student to continue work in graduate school? And if the student should decide to become a political science major, how can a teacher in that discipline intelligently advise the student what course of study to follow without knowing his level of achievement in history, economics, sociology, philosophy, and nowadays even in mathematics? In short, students' academic records are a great aid to those teachers who try to use their knowledge and experience to advise students wisely. But if a student's record is sketchy, vague, and inadequate, the advice he receives will most likely also be sketchy, vague, and inadequate.

We have already noted that grades can be a valuable guide to a student in planning for the years following his graduation, but we should note as well that grades are a valuable guide to those who must make critical decisions directly affecting a student's future plans. Graduate work usually presupposes a firm command of undergraduate work, and thus most graduate schools necessarily employ selective admission policies. Those who face the difficult task of deciding whether a particular student is to be admitted to graduate school can make that decision intelligently only if they are aware of the student's level of achievement in his various college courses, and grades are a reliable, though not infallible, measure of such achievement.

On occasion, however, it is proposed that instead of receiving an applicant's grades a graduate admissions committee receive recommendations written by each of the teachers with whom the applicant has studied. But this proposal is impractical and, even if feasible, would nevertheless be inadvisable.

The proposal is impractical for at least two reasons. First, the members of an admissions committee do not have the time to read twenty-five or thirty letters about each applicant. In the case of some of the larger professional schools, an admissions committee with twenty-five letters for each applicant would be facing more than twenty-five thousand letters and could not possibly be expected to spend the time necessary to do justice to that amount of material. Second, the large size of so many college classes makes it virtually impossible for a teacher to know each of his students personally. Thus he would be reduced to writing such conventional comments as "DeWitt is an excellent student who has mastered all of the course material" or "Davis is a fair student who has mastered some, though not much, of the course material." But what do these comments mean except that DeWitt did A work in the course and Davis did C work?

However, even if it were feasible for every one of a student's teachers to write a personalized comment about him and for an admissions committee to read all of these comments, they would not be an adequate replacement for grades. Recommendations sometimes contain valuable information, but taken by themselves they are often difficult to evaluate. A remark one teacher considers high praise may be used indiscriminately by another, and a comment employed by one teacher to express mild commendation may be used by another teacher to express mild criticism.[1] Furthermore, many recommendations are hopelessly vague and tell more about the teacher's literary style than about the academic accomplishment of the student. Thus although letters of recommendation may be helpful when used in conjunction with grades, alone they are no substitute for the relatively standardized measure of achievement grades effectively provide.

Such a standardized measure of achievement also affords a reasonable basis upon which to decide whether a student ought to be permitted to continue in school, whether he ought to be granted a college degree, and whether he ought to be awarded academic honors. These decisions, however, have all been the subject of controversy, and so we would do well to consider each of them separately.

A student who consistently does unsatisfactory work is squandering the resources of his college, wasting the time and energy of his teachers, and failing to contribute to, perhaps even interfering with, the education of his classmates. Such a student does not belong in the school he is attending, and, for the benefit of all concerned, should be asked to leave. But which students are doing unsatisfactory work? In answering this question it is clearly most sensible to rely upon the expert judgment of the faculty, and their judgment, as noted previously, is reliably reflected by a student's grades.[2]

The faculty's expertise ought also to be relied upon in deciding whether the quality of a student's work justifies his being granted a college degree. Because most students are charged tuition fees, it is tempting to conceive of a college as an educational store in which the student customers pay their money and are then entitled to a degree. But a college degree is not purchased; it is earned. It represents to the community the college's certification of a student's academic achievement, certification respected because it is backed by the expertise of the faculty. If every student who paid his tuition automatically received a degree, or if degrees were awarded by the vote of the student body, then they would become educationally meaningless and functionally worthless. In order for a college degree to retain its value and for a college education to retain its significance, the granting of degrees must be based solely upon substantial academic achievement as evaluated by recognized experts. The experts are the faculty, and their evaluations are indicated by the grades they give.

Grades also provide an effective means of determining which students are deserving of academic honors. Such honors are both an added incentive for students to pursue their work diligently and a symbol of a college's commitment to academic excellence. But in order for honors to possess such significance, they must not be granted indiscriminately or on the basis of a student's popularity. Rather, they must be awarded only to those who have attained a high level of scholarly achievement. And grades provide a standardized measure of such achievement.

Grades serve one final purpose: to motivate students to study. In the classroom, as in most areas of life, those who expect their work to be evaluated tend to do that work more assiduously. Without grades, many students might possess sufficient interest to casually peruse the course material, but few would be strongly enough concerned to devote themselves to the mastery of that material. Of course, there are a handful of students who would thoroughly study all of their course material even if they did not receive any grades. These are the saints of the academic world. But a teacher should no more assume all his students saints, than he should assume all his neighbors saints. In both cases he would do well to hope for the best but prepare for the worst. What should be remembered is that grades have helped many students who otherwise would have neglected their work, and have led some to discover for themselves the intrinsic joys of scholarship.

Chapter 8

The Case against Examinations and Grades

We must recognize that notwithstanding the many worthwhile purposes examinations and grades are intended to fulfill, much criticism has been directed against these educational tools. It has been claimed that examinations fail to provide a sound basis for evaluating a student's achievement but, instead, inhibit his independence and stifle his creativity. It has also been claimed that grades are inherently inaccurate devices which, in attempting to measure people, succeed only in traumatizing and dehumanizing them. These charges are serious, and each of them ought to be examined in detail.

Consider first the claim that examinations do not provide a sound basis for evaluating a student's achievement. Those who defend this claim argue that examinations require a student to demonstrate his knowledge under adverse conditions; he must answer a restricted set of questions within a limited amount of time, and the implicit pressure prevents many from doing their best work. Thus the results of examinations are said to be invalid.

But this line of argument overlooks the vital consideration that although examinations put pressure on students, such pressure exists whenever an individual attempts to prove to experts his competence in their field. For instance, an athlete feels pressure when he tries out for a professional team; likewise, a violinist when he auditions for an orchestral position. Pressure is inherent in such situations, for experts have high standards difficult to meet, and one must be able to meet those standards at an appointed time. The ballplayer who appears skillful in practice but plays poorly in league games lacks effective control of the requisite skills. Similarly, the student who sounds knowledgeable in conversation but performs poorly under examination conditions lacks effective control of the requisite knowledge. Thus the pressure of examinations does not invalidate the results of examinations; quite to the contrary, if there were no such pressure, the examination process would be amiss.

A second criticism of examinations is that they inhibit a student's independence, that they discourage him from pursuing topics of interest to him and instead force him to study topics of interest to his teacher. Thus, it is said, examinations impede rather than promote the learning process.

This criticism, however, rests upon the mistaken assumption that learning a particular subject matter involves nothing more than learning those aspects of the subject matter one happens to find interesting.

For example, to attain a thorough knowledge of American history, it is not sufficient to learn the history of the American Indian, no matter how interested one may be in the Indians, for American history, like any significant area of inquiry, has many important aspects, all of which must be mastered in order to attain a thorough knowledge of the field. But who is to decide which aspects of a subject matter are most important? The teacher is the recognized expert, and so he is in a position to make intelligent curricular decisions. Furthermore, the teacher's responsibility is to use his expertise to further a student's education, to guide him in studying important aspects of the subject matter he might otherwise neglect. Such guidance, in one sense, interferes with a student's independence, but in another, more significant, sense, liberates him from his own narrow preoccupations and leads him to less restricted, more independent thinking. And that, after all, is one of the essential purposes of a liberal education.

Another criticism of examinations is that they stifle a student's creativity, that they emphasize the mindless reiteration of facts and techniques instead of encouraging original, imaginative thinking about significant issues. Thus, it is said, examinations impede rather than promote the learning process.

But this criticism is mistaken for at least two reasons. First, only poor examinations emphasize learning by rote. Good examinations, as pointed out previously, place familiar material in a slightly unfamiliar light, so that in preparing for and taking examinations, students are led to develop for themselves significant connections between various aspects of the subject matter. Of course, an examination does not normally require the same degree of original, imaginative thinking required by a demanding

term paper topic. But, it must be remembered, a term
paper does not require mastery of most or even very
much of the course material; only examinations do.
In other words, the two tasks serve different purposes, and there is no point in criticizing one for not
fulfilling the purposes of the other.

The criticism in question is also mistaken because it overlooks that in order to master any significant field of inquiry, one must acquire secure control of certain fundamental information and skills.
As Whitehead wrote, "There is no getting away from
the fact that things have been found out, and that to
be effective in the modern world you must have a core
of definite acquirement of the best practice. To write
poetry you must study metre: and to build bridges you
must be learned in the strength of material. Even the
Hebrew prophets had learned to write, probably in
those days requiring no mean effort. The untutored
art of genius is—in the words of the Prayer Book—a
vain thing, fondly invented."[1] It is simply unrealistic
to suppose that original, imaginative thinking of a
sustained and productive sort flows from the minds of
those ignorant of the fundamental information and
skills related to their field of inquiry. It has been said
that the mark of a knowledgeable person is not what
he knows, but whether he is adept at looking up what
he needs to know. But if this were so, then the most
knowledgeable people in the world would be librarians. A person who lacks fundamental information
and skills is not in a position to understand and intelligently evaluate material confronting him, so he is
unable to connect ideas in the ways necessary for
sustained, productive thinking. And even if, as is
highly doubtful, such an individual had the time to
research everything he needed to know, he would not
know what to research, for he would not be aware of

all he needed to know. But how can it be determined whether an individual possesses the fundamental information and skills related to his field of inquiry? Examinations enable both teacher and student to make such determinations effectively, and thus, rather than stifling creativity, help to provide the framework within which original, imaginative thinking can be most productive.

Turning now from criticisms of examinations to criticisms of grades, consider first the claim that grades are inherently inaccurate. Those who defend this position argue that the same paper would be graded differently by different instructors, and therefore a student's grade is not a reliable measure of his achievement but merely indicates the particular bias of his instructor.

However, a student's work is generally not judged with significant difference by different instructors. In fact, teachers in the same discipline usually agree as to which students are doing outstanding work, which are doing good work, which are doing fair work, which are doing poor work, and which are doing unsatisfactory work (or no work at all).[2] Of course, two competent instructors may offer divergent evaluations of the same piece of work. But the fact that experts sometimes disagree is not reason to assume there is no such thing as expertise. For example, two competent doctors may offer divergent diagnoses of the same condition, but their disagreement does not imply that doctors' diagnoses are in general biased and unreliable. Similarly, two competent art critics may offer divergent evaluations of the same work of art, but such a disagreement does not imply that a critic's evaluations are usually biased and unreliable. Inevitably, experts, like all human beings, will sometimes disagree about complex judgments, but we would be foolish to allow such disagreements to obscure the obvious fact that in any established field of inquiry some individuals are knowledgeable and others are not. And clearly the opinions of those who are knowledgeable are the most reliable measure of an individual's achievement in that field. Thus, although teachers sometimes disagree, they are knowledgeable individuals whose grades represent a reliable measure of a student's level of achievement.

A second criticism of grades is that they traumatize students. Those who support this criticism argue that grades foster competition, arousing a bitterness and hostility which transform an otherwise tranquil academic atmosphere into a pressure-filled, nerve-wracking situation unsuited for genuine learning. In such a situation, it is said, students are more worried about obtaining good grades than about obtaining a good education.

But this criticism emphasizes the possibly harmful effects of competition while overlooking its beneficial effects. Often only by competing with others do we bring out the best in ourselves. As Gilbert Highet once noted, "It is sad, sometimes, to see a potentially brilliant pupil slouching through his work, sulky and willful, wasting his time and thought on trifles, because he has no real equals in his own class; and it is heartening to see how quickly, when a rival is transferred from another section or enters from another school, the first boy will find a fierce joy in learning and a real purpose in life." [3] In short, competition fosters excellence, and without that challenge most of us would be satisfied with accomplishing far less than we are capable of.

However, even if competition did not have beneficial effects, it would still be an inherent part of academic life, just as it is an inherent part of so many aspects of life. Many people have the same goals, but only comparatively few can achieve them. For example, not everyone who so desires can be a surgeon, a lawyer, an engineer, or a professional football player. Thus competition arises. And since academic success is desired not only for its own sake but also because it relates to success in many other competitive fields, competition will always exist in academic life.

The question then is not whether competition should be eliminated from the academic sphere, but how it can be channeled so as to maximize beneficial effects and minimize potentially harmful effects. The key to this difficult task lies in encouraging each student to strive as vigorously as possible to fulfill his own potential, in praising his efforts when he tries his hardest, and in appealing to his sense of pride when his energies flag. Treating him so does not lead him to emphasize good grades rather than a good education, for he cannot achieve a good education without striving for mastery of subject matter. And if grades are awarded as they should be, on the basis of accurate measures of a student's level of achievement, then they will indicate his mastery of subject matter. Thus a student concerned with grades is concerned with a prime component of a good education.

A third criticism of grades is that in attempting to measure people, they succeed only in dehumanizing and categorizing them, depriving them of their uniqueness, and reducing them to a letter of the alphabet. Thus, it is said, grades defeat one of the essential purposes of an education: to aid each individual in developing his individuality.

A grade, however, is not and is not intended to be

a measure of a person. It is, rather, a measure of a person's level of achievement in a particular course of study. To give a student a C in an introductory physics course is not to say that the student is a C person with a C personality or C moral character, only that he is a person with a C level of achievement in introductory physics.

Grades no more reduce students to letters than batting averages reduce baseball players to numbers. That Ted Williams had a lifetime batting average of .344 and Joe Garagiola an average of .257 does not mean Williams is a better person than Garagiola, but only that Williams was a better hitter. And why does it dehumanize either man to recognize that one was a better hitter than the other?

Indeed, to recognize an individual's strengths and weaknesses, to know his areas of expertise, his areas of competence, and his areas of ignorance is not to deny but to emphasize his individuality. If Delaney and Delancey are known to their teachers only as two faces in the classroom, then their comparative anonymity is apt to lead to their individual differences being overlooked. But if Delaney has a reputation as an excellent history student with a weakness in mathematics, while Delancey is known as a generally poor student, but one who has a gift for creative writing, then these two students are no longer anonymous cogs in a machine, and their education can be tailored to suit their needs. Thus grades do not dehumanize an individual; on the contrary, they contribute to a recognition of his uniqueness and to the possible development of his individual interests and abilities.

Yet there is one further challenge to the entire system of examinations and grades, for as was pointed out earlier, this system places important decisions affecting students' lives in the hands of those comparatively unaffected by these decisions and perhaps quite uninterested in making them. Such a situation is indeed hazardous, and the potential problems are compounded by the difficulty of constructing and applying suitable examination and grading procedures. Of course, suitable procedures are the ones most likely to fulfill the worthwhile purposes examinations and grades are intended to serve, and we have already seen what those are. But what specifically are the procedures most likely to fulfill those purposes?

Chapter 9

Testing and Grading

Constructing a good examination is a creative endeavor, and, as in the case of all creative endeavors, there are no surefire formulas for success; the most one can reasonably hope for are broad guidelines to provide a sound basis for at least partial success. The first such guideline is that an examination should be representative of the course material. Consider, for instance, a course in the history of modern philosophy that devotes two or three weeks to the study of each of six philosophers: Descartes, Leibniz, Locke, Berkeley, Hume, and Kant. If the final examination is to serve its proper function as a test of the scope and depth of a student's knowledge of the course material, then the examination should be structured so that a student is called upon to demonstrate considerable knowledge about all six of the authors studied. The examination would be unsatisfactory if it tested only a student's general philosophical ability, not his knowledge of the six authors studied, or if it tested a student's knowledge of only one or two authors studied and permitted him to neglect the others. For whatever such unsatisfactory examinations might be intended to test, they would fail to test adequately the scope and depth of a student's knowledge of the history of modern philosophy.

Of course, an examination representative of the course material need not deny students a choice as to which examination questions they wish to answer. Such a choice is an attractive feature of an examination, since it allows students an opportunity to demonstrate their special interests and abilities. But the crucial point is that such choices should be so arranged that a student's answers will adequately reflect his knowledge of the entire course material. And if certain course material is so essential that all students should be familiar with it, then no choice should be given. For contrary to common practice, students need not always be offered a choice of examination questions. What they should be offered is an examination representative of the course material.

A second guideline for constructing good examinations is posing questions that require detailed answers. Perhaps the most serious fault of college examinations is that they allow a student to talk around the subject matter without ever having to demonstrate more than a superficial knowledge of the course material. Again in contrast to common practice, much can be said in favor of questions that have answers, answers to be found in or at least closely related to the course readings. An examination lacking such questions is not merely a poor test of a student's knowledge but leads him to suppose that thorough knowledge of the course material amounts to no more than knowing a few stray bits of information strung together by some vague generalizations about some even vaguer concepts. Such an examination is worse than no examination at all; it is an educational travesty that leads a student to suppose he has mastered material about which he knows virtually nothing.

But the fact that examination questions ought to require detailed answers is no reason why students should be overwhelmed with true-false or multiple-choice questions. Although these can sometimes be of educational value, unless they are well constructed and appropriate to the aims of the course, they turn the examination into a guessing game that stresses knowledge of minutiae rather than the understanding of fundamental concepts and principles. For instance, only a foolish examination in the history of modern philosophy would be filled with questions such as "The title of Section IX of Hume's *An Enquiry Concerning Human Understanding* is (a) Of Liberty and Necessity, (b) Of the Reason of Animals, (c) Of Miracles, (d) All of the above, (e) None of the above." On the other hand it would be equally foolish for such an examination to be filled with questions such as "Does it seem to you that anything in the work of Kant helps us to understand ourselves?" What is needed is neither a trivial nor vague question but a sharply defined, significant, challenging question, one such as: "Both Descartes and Berkeley raise doubts about the existence of the material world. Compare and contrast (1) the arguments they use to raise these doubts, and (2) their conclusions concerning the possible resolution of these doubts." An examination with questions such as this not only provides a rigorous test of a student's knowledge but also clearly indicates to the student that mastery of the subject matter is a demanding enterprise, requiring far more intellectual effort than the memorization of trivia or the improvisation of hazy, high-flown vacuities.

If an examination adheres to the two important guidelines just discussed, then there is reason to suppose it will fulfill the worthwhile purposes it should serve. However, several other pitfalls must be avoided in order for an examination to be as effective as possible. First, the examination should not be so long that most students are more worried about finishing than about providing the best possible answers. Of course, if a student takes too long to answer a question, it is clear he does not have secure enough control of the required material. But basically an examination should not be a race against time; it should be constructed so a student working at a normal pace has sufficient time to read the questions carefully, compose his thoughts, write his answers legibly, and reread his work to make corrections. No matter how well-constructed examination questions may be, if there is not sufficient time to answer them thoughtfully, the examination will turn into a shambles and be of little use to anyone.

A second pitfall to be avoided is the omission of clear directions at the top of the examination paper. Imagine sitting down to begin work and reading the following directions: "Answer three questions from Part I and two questions from Part II, but do not answer questions 2, 3, and 6 unless you also answer question 9. Question 1 is required, unless you answer questions 3 and 5." By the time a student has fully understood these directions and decided which questions he ought to answer, he will already be short of time.

When a student sits down to take an examination, he is understandably tense and liable to misread the directions, answer the wrong questions, and bungle the examination. If he does so, the fault is probably not his, for the teacher has the responsibility to make the directions so clear that the student will find them virtually impossible to misunderstand. A teacher has sufficient time to work out clear directions, and he owes it to his students to provide such directions. The examination should be a test of a student's knowledge of the course material, not a test of his ability to solve verbal puzzles.

A third pitfall is the failure to inform students of the relative importance of each answer in the grading of the examination. Suppose a student begins work on an examination in which he is required to answer three questions, but is not told the teacher considers the answer to the third question more important than the combined answers to the first two. The student will probably spend an equal amount of time on each, never realizing he should concentrate his time and effort on the third. But his mistake indicates no lack of knowledge on his part. It is simply a result of the teacher's keeping his own intentions a secret. And this secret serves no other function than to distort the results of the examination. It is only fair that a student be informed as to how many points each question is worth, so that he can plan his work accordingly.

One final pitfall must be avoided in order for an examination to fulfill its proper purposes, and this pitfall relates not to the construction of the examination, but to its grading. A teacher is responsible for grading examinations as carefully and fairly as possible. To do otherwise is to waste much of the effort put into constructing and taking the examination, for an examination graded carelessly or unfairly does not provide an accurate measure of a student's knowledge. While the most essential element in the proper grading of examination papers is the teacher's serious effort to carry out his responsibility conscientiously, many teachers have found a few simple suggestions about grading techniques helpful.

First, a teacher should grade papers without knowing whose paper he is grading. An answer from a student who does generally good work may seem more impressive than the same answer from a student who does generally poor work. Next, it is best not to grade a paper by reading it from start to finish but to read and grade all students' answers to one question at a time. This procedure ensures that a teacher will pay attention to each answer a student gives and not skim the paper after reading only the first one or two answers carefully. Furthermore, correcting papers in this way makes much less likely the possibility a teacher will alter his standards as he moves from one paper to another, for it is far easier to stabilize standards for answers to the same question than for entire examination papers. Finally, before grading a question, a teacher should list for himself the major points he expects students to mention in their answers. He can then check each essay against this list, providing yet another safeguard against altering standards as he moves from one paper to another. And such a list also provides a teacher with the means to justify his grades, since he is in a position to indicate to students what a good answer should be. Such information makes clear that grades have not been meted out arbitrarily and also aids each student in achieving both a better understanding of the material tested and an increased awareness of his own strengths and weaknesses. In order for such information to be most useful, examinations should be graded, returned to students, and discussed in class as soon as possible.

Examinations that adhere to these guidelines and avoid these pitfalls are almost sure to be reasonably successful. It should be kept in mind, however, that good examinations reinforce one another, since each one a student takes guides him in future study. Thus if he takes a number of good examinations in a single course, as that course proceeds he learns how to derive the greatest possible benefit from his study time. Multiple examinations in a single course also serve to discourage students from the popular but disastrous policy of wasting almost the entire term and then cramming for one final examination. The more frequent the examinations, the less need for cramming. Thus it is not, as some have said, that examinations encourage cramming. Infrequent examinations encourage cramming. Frequent examinations encourage studying. And good examinations encourage useful studying.

Having now discussed suitable examination procedures, we should next consider suitable grading procedures. Much discussion has taken place about alternative grading systems, but the basic principle for constructing an effective grading system remains quite simple: it should contain the maximum number of grade levels teachers can use consistently. A grading system should be as specific as possible because grades serve as a guide for the educational decisions of both students and faculty; up to a reasonable point the more detailed the guide is, the more helpful it is. If a student's academic record is sketchy and vague, then most likely he will have a sketchy, vague idea of his own abilities and accomplishments and will be hindered in his attempts to assess his past efforts, evaluate his present capabilities, and formulate his future plans. And not only will he himself be hindered, but those who try to advise him or evaluate his accomplishments will be at a serious disadvantage. It is just not sufficient to know that Kubersky passed a course. Was he an A student, a strong B student, a weak C student, or a D student? Without an answer to this question, neither Kubersky nor anyone else knows much about his level of achievement.

But there is a limit to how specific a grading system should be. Ultimately we reach a point where no reasonable basis exists for deciding whether a student's work is at one level or another. There is little sense, for example, in trying to decide whether an English composition should receive a grade of 86.32 or 86.31, for no teacher can consistently differentiate between work on these two levels.

The question is then, using the principle that a grading system should contain the maximum number of grade levels teachers can use consistently, how many such grade levels should there be? My own experience has led me to believe that in college the most effective grading system is the traditional one, consisting of ten symbols: A, A−, B+, B, B−, C+, C, C−, D, F. This ten-level system is specific enough to provide the needed information about a student's level of achievement while enabling teachers to differentiate consistently between work on any two of the ten levels. Borderline cases will sometimes arise, but the distinction between work on any two levels is clear, despite the possibility of borderline cases, just as the distinction between bald men and hirsute men is clear, despite the possibility of borderline cases.

Perhaps the most controversial aspect of the traditional ten-level system is its grade of F, for many have claimed that if a student knows he will have a failure permanently on his record, he may become so discouraged he will give up on his education altogether. In order to preclude such a possibility it has been proposed that the grade of F be replaced by a grade of NC (No Credit), which would indicate to the registrar both that the student should receive no credit for the course and that his transcript should show no record of his having taken the course.

Such a grade, however, would obviously be pure deception, for the student *did* take the course and he failed to master any significant part of it. If he should take the same course again and pass it, his transcript should indicate as much. Otherwise, those who are trying to evaluate his work will be misled, since it is likely that a student who had to take introductory chemistry two, three, or four times before passing lacks the scientific or study skills of someone who passed the course on his first try. It is not a tragedy to fail a course, but it is a failure, and we must learn from failures, not give them another name and pretend they did not occur. Indeed, one mark of a mature individual is facing up to and taking responsibility for failures. As a colleague of mine once remarked during a faculty meeting in which the NC grade was being discussed: "When I die and stand before the Heavenly Judge in order to have my life evaluated, it may be that I will receive a grade of F. But let it not be said that my life was a 'No Credit.'"

A suitable grading system, however, does not ensure suitable grading, for unless the system is used properly, grades will not achieve the worthwhile purposes they are intended to serve. And, unfortunately, improper uses of the system are all too common.

One such misuse is to award grades on bases other than a student's level of achievement in the course work. Irrelevant bases for grades include a student's sex, race, religion, nationality, physical appearance, dress, personality, attitudes, innate capacities, and previous academic record. None of these factors should even be considered in awarding grades. To repeat what was said earlier, a grade ought not to be a measure of a person; it ought to be a measure of a person's level of achievement in a particular course of study, and the only reasonable basis for measuring this is the quality of work which he does in that course.

The most effective way for a teacher to assure his students that no extraneous factors will enter into the awarding of grades is to state clearly at the outset of the term exactly how final grades will be determined. How much will the final examination count? How much will short quizzes count? How about the term paper and other shorter papers? Will laboratory work count? Will a student's participation in class discussion be a factor? By answering these questions at the very beginning of the course, a teacher sets a student's mind at ease and, in addition, enables him to concentrate his time and effort on the most important aspects of the course. Of course, some teachers assume that if they do not discuss their grading policy, the students will not worry about grades. But quite to the contrary, a teacher's failure to discuss his grading policy increases uncertainty and worry and furthermore provides no guidance as to how the students should work to do their best and get the most out of the course. And, after all, such guidance is precisely what the teacher is expected to provide.

A second obvious misuse of the grading system, exceedingly rare nowadays, results from the reluctance of some teachers to award high grades. Such teachers pride themselves on how rarely they give an

A or B, and how frequently they give C's, D's, or F's. But low grading is a foolish source of pride, for such grading suggests the teacher is unable to recognize good work when he sees it. That a student's work does not deserve immortal fame is no reason it does not deserve an A. Just as a third-grade student who receives an A in writing need not be the literary equal of a college student who receives an A in English composition, so a college student who receives an A in English composition need not be the literary equal of Jonathan Swift or Bertrand Russell. Giving a student an A in a course does not mean he has learned everything there is to know about course material or that he is as knowledgeable as his teacher; giving a student an A simply means that, considering what could reasonably be expected, the student has done excellent work. If a third-grade teacher rarely gives an A or a B, his principal does not assume this teacher always has poor students in his classes. He assumes, rather, that this teacher has a distorted sense of academic values. A similar conclusion should be reached about a college teacher who rarely gives an A or a B. Such a teacher is misapplying the grading symbols and preventing grades from fulfilling their important educational functions.

A third misuse of the grading system, one especially prevalent today, results from the reluctance of many teachers to award low grades. These instructors pride themselves on never giving students a hard time or underestimating the value of a student's efforts. But high grading, like low grading, is a foolish source of pride; it suggests that the teacher is unable to recognize poor work when he sees it. Not to differentiate between two students, one doing poor or unsatisfactory work and one doing fair work, is a subtle form of discrimination against the better student.

Giving a student a D or an F in a course does not mean that the student is a foolish or evil person; the low grade simply means that, considering what could reasonably be expected, the student has done poor or unsatisfactory work. If a third-grade teacher rarely gives low grades, his principal does not assume this teacher has the school's most brilliant students. The principal assumes, rather, that this teacher is giving his seal of approval to incompetent work. A similar conclusion should be reached about a college teacher who rarely gives low grades. Such a teacher, like the teacher who rarely gives high grades, is misapplying the grading symbols and preventing grades from fulfilling their functions.[1]

A fourth and final misuse of the grading system is the practice commonly referred to as "grading on a curve." The essence of this widely adopted practice is deciding what percentage of students in a class will receive a particular grade, without considering the level of work actually done by any of the students. For example, a teacher may decide before a course ever begins that 10 percent of the students will receive an A, 20 percent a B, 40 percent a C, 20 percent a D, and 10 percent an F. Distributing grades in this way produces an aesthetically pleasing curve on a graph, but the procedure is invalid, for how well a student has learned a particular subject matter does not depend upon how well his fellow students have learned the same subject matter. Perhaps in many large classes approximately 10 percent of the students actually do A work and a similar percentage F work, but this fact is no reason at all why in any specific class exactly 10 percent of the students must receive an A and another 10 percent must receive an F. Suppose 25 percent of the students in a class do excellent work and 5 percent unsatisfactory work; then the 25 percent should receive an A and the 5 percent an F.

Or suppose 5 percent of the students in a class do excellent work and 25 percent do unsatisfactory work; then the 5 percent should receive an A and the 25 percent should receive an F. For the grade a student receives is not to be a measure of his rank in class; it is to be a measure of his level of achievement in a particular course of study. And although judging a student's level of achievement does depend upon considering what can reasonably be expected of him, such a judgment does not and should not depend upon the level of achievement of other students who happen to be taking the same course simultaneously. Since the Procrustean practice of grading on a curve rests upon such irrelevant considerations, the practice ought to be abandoned.

But even if a teacher is cognizant of appropriate procedures, how can it be ensured he will apply them conscientiously? There is, of course, no practical way to ensure that anyone, whether doctor, journalist, or taxi driver, will do his job conscientiously. A chairman has the responsibility to make certain no member of his department is guilty of gross negligence. But, ultimately, a teacher must decide for himself whether to be conscientious. If he is deeply committed to maintaining high academic standards, he will be willing to spend the time and effort required to make the most effective possible use of examinations and grades. But if he is unconcerned about promoting excellence and is satisfied with exalting mediocrity, he will be unwilling to give of himself in order to provide his students with effective examinations and accurate grades. What no teacher must be allowed to forget, however, is that if he chooses to ignore proper examination and grading procedures both his students and his society will be the losers.

Chapter 10

The Authority
of a Teacher

Even after plausible arguments have been offered in defense of examinations and grades, the very
idea of these educational tools still offends some
people. It would be easy to suppose that such negative
reaction is based on nothing more than unhappy experiences suffered at the hands of incompetent
teachers. But far more is at issue than can be
adequately dealt with by such *ad hominem* considerations. For examinations and grades are reminders of
a teacher's authority, and understandably the notion
of authority may raise the specter of brutal political
authoritarianism.

But authority itself is neither good nor evil.
What is crucial is the purpose for which it is exercised
and the manner in which it is employed. A conductor

must have authority over his orchestra; a pilot must have authority over his crew; a surgeon must have authority over his operating team. In each case, the authority should be limited in appropriate ways, and safeguards are needed against malfeasance. But the responsibilities of conductors, pilots, and surgeons require them to have authority. Without it they could not properly carry out their duties.

Interestingly, we speak not only of authority as power but also of *an* authority, that is, an expert. And these two concepts are related, for often the responsibilities that entail the exercise of authority or power are assigned to an individual in virtue of his presumed authority or expertise. Such is the case with teachers, for it makes sense to give an individual pedagogic responsibility only if he possesses superior knowledge. If a person understands a subject no better than you do, why should he be your teacher?

An instructor's obligation is to guide the learning process. He is expected to know which material should be studied and in what order it should be presented. He is expected to know how each individual should proceed so that his efforts will be most productive. He is expected to know what constitutes progress and the extent to which each student has achieved it. Students themselves do not have such knowledge; that is why they are students.

Imagine yourself taking a beginning bridge lesson and hearing your instructor inquire whether you would prefer to study finesses or analyze the Vienna Coup. Such a question would be senseless, for a reasonable answer depends upon some knowledge of bridge, and if you already had that, you wouldn't be a beginner.

It would be equally inane for your instructor to decide your skill at bidding by asking you to evaluate yourself. For sensible judgments of this sort depend upon an expert's insight, and it is your instructor, not you, who is supposed to be the expert. If he himself doesn't know how good your bidding is, he shouldn't be your instructor.

Unfortunately some teachers, like some members of any vocation, seek to avoid their responsibilities, and a common method of doing so is passing the buck to students. I recall a former colleague telling me that his class in the history of modern philosophy was going to jump from Leibniz to Kant, leaving out the empiricists, Locke, Berkeley, and Hume. When I inquired why he was proceeding so oddly, he replied that he had taken a vote of his students and they had preferred not to read the empiricists.

The truth was that this instructor, knowing little about the empiricists, wanted to omit them but didn't want to be held accountable for such an obvious gap in the course. So he tried to absolve himself of responsibility by describing the empiricists in wholly negative terms and then asking his students which material they preferred to read. Obviously he could have persuaded them of virtually anything, for as far as they knew, Locke, Berkeley, and Hume might have been the outfield for the 1914 Boston Braves.

A teacher is properly held responsible for what is going on in the classroom, and thus he must possess the authority to direct the course. To speak of a teacher's authority, however, is not to suggest that he should act in an authoritarian manner, exercising complete control over the will of his students. The appropriate relationship is that of guide, not god.

A useful parallel can be drawn with the proper relationship of a doctor to his patients. A good doctor pays close attention to his patient's reactions and adapts his treatment to the individual case. But if he is required to prescribe medicine he believes to be inappropriate, he refuses to do so, for he himself is responsible for the prescriptions he signs. And if he is called upon to certify a patient's health, he does so on the basis of generally recognized criteria, not on the basis of the patient's own criteria.

The situation is similar to that of a good teacher. He pays close attention to his student's reactions and adapts his instruction to the individual case. But if he is requested to discuss material in a way he believes inappropriate, he refuses to do so, for he himself is responsible for the course he is offering. And if he is called upon to certify a student's competence, he does so on the basis of generally recognized standards, not on the basis of the student's own criteria.

The authority of a teacher may be threatened in various ways, the most flagrant of which is the attempt to dictate the opinions he must espouse. The tenure system, which I shall discuss later, is a defense against that menace. But a more subtle yet equally serious threat is posed by the increasingly widespread practice of judging an instructor's pedagogic skill primarily on the basis of evaluations prepared by his students.

Nothing is amiss about consulting students as a convenient source for such easily verifiable matters as whether a teacher holds class regularly, whether he returns examinations without delay, whether he provides detailed comments on term papers, and whether he is available for consultation outside the classroom. Indeed, students should be encouraged to complain about a teacher who shirks such elementary responsibilities.

But students are not in position to judge whether a teacher is presenting his material competently or whether years after graduation his methods of instruction will prove valuable. Students know if a teacher is likeable but not if he is knowledgeable; they know if his lectures are enjoyable, but not if they are reliable.

Typical of the wrong sort of question to ask students is one I remember seeing on an evaluation form: "Does the instructor discuss recent developments in the field?" How are students expected to know the source of the information with which they are provided? And even if something is described to them as a recent development in the field, they are still in the dark as to whether that material is, in fact, either recent or a significant development.

Several years ago an experiment was carried out to test the hypothesis that learners may be seriously mistaken about their teacher's competence. A distinguished-looking professional actor who sounded authoritative was selected to present a lecture to several groups of highly trained educators, among them psychiatrists, psychologists, and social workers. They were told they would be hearing a talk by Dr. Myron L. Fox, said to be an authority on the application of mathematics to human behavior. His address was titled, "Mathematical Game Theory as Applied to Physician Education." The actor was coached "to present his topic and conduct his question and answer period with an excessive use of double talk, neologisms, non sequiturs, and contradictory statements. All this was to be interspersed with parenthetical humor and meaningless references to unrelated topics."[1]

At the end of the one-hour lecture and subsequent half-hour discussion, a questionnaire was distributed to the listeners, inquiring what they thought of Dr. Fox. Here are some of their responses:

Excellent presentation, enjoyed listening. Has warm manner. Good flow, seems enthusiastic. Lively examples. Extremely articulate. Good analysis of subject that has been personally studied before. He was certainly captivating. Knowledgeable.

My favorite reply was offered by one individual who found the presentation "too intellectual." Interestingly, all the listeners had significantly more favorable than unfavorable responses, and not a single one saw through the hoax. The author's conclusion is that "student satisfaction with learning may represent little more than the illusion of having learned."

I once noticed on a college bulletin board an announcement of a meeting that had been called by students to demand a greater role in the evaluation of faculty. The sign proclaimed, "The Administration Must Think We're Stupid." But, as is clear from the Dr. Fox case, what is at issue is not the brainpower of students but their expertise in particular subject matter. Those educators who were fooled by the actor were surely intelligent, but knowing little about the material he was supposedly discussing, they were in no position to evaluate his performance.

The most reliable method of judging an instructor's skill is for him to be observed in his classroom by various faculty members from the same discipline, chosen on the basis of their outstanding teaching performance throughout many years. Of course, some instructors object to any visits from professional colleagues, but why should those instructors be willing, as virtually all are, to allow into their classroom auditors, friends or relatives of students, and even faculty members from other departments, while locking their doors against those most qualified to understand what is going on? Admittedly, no human judges are infallible, but surely it makes sense to prefer those who are competent.

However, for a teacher to be evaluated primarily

on the basis of student opinion is not merely inappropriate, it is also dangerous. For as Charles Frankel has observed, "Teaching is a professional relationship, not a popularity contest. To invite students to participate in the selection or promotion of their teachers . . . exposes the teacher to intimidation."[2]

But it is vital that a teacher not be frightened of his students, for he is expected to question their pet beliefs, expose their prejudices, challenge them with demanding tests, and evaluate their work rigorously. A teacher afraid of his students might as well pack his briefcase and go home, for he cannot educate those he fears. Seeking to propitiate students, granting them favors in exchange for their support, is disgraceful, and no one should be put in a position that encourages such shameful conduct.

A teacher's authority must be respected and protected. Without it, he cannot be expected to carry out his responsibilities, and, surprising as it may seem to some, the first victims of his incapacity are those he is supposed to be instructing.

Chapter 11

Requirements

We expect the faculty of a medical school to require all candidates for an M.D. degree to learn anatomy. We expect the faculty of a law school to require all candidates for a J.D. degree to learn contracts. Which subjects should we expect the faculty of a liberal arts college to require of all candidates for a B.A. degree?

Here is one answer, found in a 1960s' college catalogue:

> Competent writing and reading are essential to all other studies and for most occupations in later life; therefore a basic course in English fundamentals is given in the freshman year. This course is followed by one in the literature of Western Europe, introducing the student to his literary heritage. European culture is explored further in a one-term course in the history and literature of Greece and Rome.

A full-year history course then surveys the major developments—political, social, economic, and cultural—that mark the changing fortunes of European civilization from the decline of Rome to the present. A one-term course in philosophical analysis acquaints the student with the great philosophical systems in Western culture and introduces him to the techniques of philosophical thinking.

Because of the interest in the arts and because of their place in the development of civilization, students take a year-long course in the history of either music or art.

International communication in all fields of knowledge, as well as in political and business relations, has become increasingly important and urgent. In consequence, the College requires that before graduation every student should have a reasonable command of one foreign language.

Four one-term courses in the social sciences introduce the student to sociology, the picture of the social structure in which we live; psychology, the study of human experience and behavior; government, the theory, operation, and politics of the American political system compared with other systems; and economics, the study of how men make a living.

Science and mathematics are essential parts of a modern liberal arts education; the basic values inherent in both go far beyond the practical significance attained by them in modern times. The science segment of the program is designed to give the student these values without, however, inserting the detail needed by the specialist. The sequence begins with a one-term course in mathematics, followed by a term of physical science. The student then pursues a one-term laboratory course in either biology, chemistry, geology or physics.[1]

Here is a second answer, taken from a 1960s' catalogue of another college:

College Composition (one year). First term: intensive training in the composition of expository and argumentative essays. Topics are based upon readings in 19th- and 20th-century authors. Second term: development of a long paper; introduction to methods of research and the use of the library; discovery of some of the resources of the English language through a study of its poetry.

Contemporary Civilization (two years). First year: "Development of Western Institutions and Social Ideas." A study of the major political, economic, and philosophical influences that have shaped the character of Western civilization.

Second year: "Man in Contemporary Society." A study of those problems and issues basic to an understanding of contemporary society, as reflected by leading ideas and important thinkers in modern social science.

Humanities (two years). First year: "Masterpieces of European Literature and Philosophy." Works are studied in chronological sequence and almost every work is read in its entirety. Works by Homer, Herodotus, Thucydides, Aeschylus, Sophocles, Euripides, Aristophanes, Plato, Aristotle, Lucretius, Vergil, the books of Genesis and Job, books of the New Testament, works by Augustine, Dante, Rabelais, Montaigne, Shakespeare, Cervantes, Milton, Spinoza, Molière, Swift, Voltaire, Goethe, and Dostoevsky.

Second year: "Masterpieces of the Fine Arts." Discussion and analysis of the artistic qualities and significance of selected works of art, such as the Parthenon in Athens, the Gothic cathedral, the sculpture of Michelangelo, the paintings of Rembrandt. "Masterpieces of Music." Performance, analysis, and discussion of representative works from the 16th century to the present.

Mathematics-Science (two years). One two-term course from each of two of the following groups: mathematics; astronomy, chemistry, physics; botany, geology, psychology, zoology.

Foreign Language. Completion of the second-year (intermediate) College course with a grade of B− or better, or completion of the first term of the third-year (advanced) College course with a passing grade.[2]

Here is a third answer, adopted as official policy by numerous colleges during the 1970s: None.

A rationale for answers similar to the first two was provided earlier in the book, but on what basis could anyone seriously defend the view that candidates for a B. A. degree need not master any specific subjects at all? Has a revolution in man's understanding of the world subverted the importance of the sciences, social sciences, and humanities?

Of course not. At virtually every school, teachers still advise, urge, even cajole students to take a wide variety of traditional courses. But many faculty members now consider requirements anathema, believing their imposition to be an act of repression and thus inconsistent with the ideals of a free society.

But this line of reasoning overlooks the crucial fact that not all restrictions are repressive. Consider, for example, the law that requires motorists to stop at red lights. This rule restricts or limits drivers but surely does not repress or enslave them, for by contributing to sensible order on the road, it enables all to proceed safely in whatever direction they choose. A free society should strive to preserve fundamental rights and eliminate repression, but abolishing all social and institutional restrictions would lead only to an anarchy in which no liberties were secured.

Universities within a democracy should be especially concerned to avoid acts of repression, for their mission is the pursuit and transmission of knowledge, and that task is impossible without freedom of inquiry. However, a university that places no restrictions on students and automatically awards all of them diplomas will soon debase its degree and collapse into educational chaos.

To support requirements is not to deny individuality. Obviously, people differ in their capacities and interests; what stimulates one individual may stultify another. A democracy should recognize such differences and show equal consideration for all persons by encouraging each to enjoy his own distinctive growth. As John Stuart Mill wrote, "In proportion to the development of his individuality, each person becomes more valuable to himself, and is, therefore, capable of being more valuable to others."[3]

But just as we should realize the importance of

promoting individuality, so we should recognize the benefits to be derived from all citizens possessing certain attributes in common. We are all in need of good health care, we are all in need of a reasonable income, and we are all in need of the knowledge that enables us to carry out our responsibilities as members of a free society. The diversity that is the pride of a democracy is in no way enhanced by anyone's being sick, poor, or ignorant.

Opponents of a structured curriculum are apt to claim that no one can learn anything in a required course. But although this view is often presented as if it were obviously true, it is, in fact, obviously false.

During my undergraduate years at Columbia College, everyone took the required courses in the history of art and the history of music. Needless to say, students often approached these subjects without much enthusiasm. Many, however, finding themselves for the first time at an art gallery or a concert, suddenly developed a keen interest, even a lifelong passion, for the arts. Their experience, by no means unusual, refutes the claim that nothing can be learned in a required course.

Indeed, years after leaving school, many college graduates find as much or greater value in courses that had been required outside their major as in those chosen within it. For undergraduate work in one's speciality is often superseded by graduate or professional work in the same discipline, but a course in an unfamiliar area may well be the only occasion in an entire lifetime for systematic study of an important field of human endeavor.

Admittedly, not everyone who takes a required course enjoys the experience. But not everyone who takes an elective course enjoys that experience. Nor is enjoyment the be-all and end-all of education.

However, those who teach a required course should be especially concerned to motivate their students. For such a course is supposed to be important to all, regardless of their initial interest, and an instructor should present his material so as to exhibit that importance even to the skeptical, thereby engaging each learner's interest and enriching the educational process.

Fear of this pedagogic challenge is another reason some faculty members oppose required courses. They prefer to teach a subject only to those already interested in it.

But helping a person acquire a liberal education often involves broadening his interests, leading him to recognize the value of subjects that may have been mangled or omitted during his earlier years. For instance, a student majoring in biology who sees no point in studying history, literature, or philosophy needs to acquire greater understanding of these fields, and a faculty that cares about his education will ensure that he obtains what he needs, even if it would be less bothersome to allow him to study only biology. Neglected needs are likely to become weaknesses, and the weaknesses of individuals contribute to the weakness of a democratic society. While it is easier to teach those who are eager to learn, the aims of liberal education are not necessarily served by catering to the faculty's comfort.

Some who object to college-wide requirements do so on the supposition that virtually all students will select a sensible distribution of courses regardless of what rules the faculty may prescribe.

The evidence, however, does not support this utopian view. It has been demonstrated on countless occasions that when, for example, a school abolishes its foreign language or science requirement, registration in these demanding courses plummets. But such facts should not be surprising, for how many of us will choose an arduous route if a far less demanding one is available?

Interestingly, few of those who oppose requiring a student to take courses in areas far removed from his major would be willing to abolish requirements within majors. It is generally agreed that a mathematics major must study calculus and a music major must study harmony. Why then the opposition to requirements for a liberal education?

Since faculty members are specialists in particular disciplines, not in the totality of the curriculum, each tends to assume that his colleagues have a clear sense of what is involved in mastering their own subjects but not of what is involved in acquiring a liberal education. At a faculty meeting few will object if the physics department wishes all its majors to study mechanics, but an uproar is likely if the physicists urge that all students should be required to study science.

What is often overlooked, however, is that each faculty member's expertise puts him in the best possible position to determine how aspects of his own and related subjects may contribute to the content of a liberal education. The collective wisdom of the faculty is thus the appropriate source of the vision needed to establish degree requirements.[4]

A faculty unwilling to take responsibility for such curricular decisions has no right to award diplomas. If its members are unable to enumerate the components of a liberal education, they cannot reasonably decide who has earned a B.A. degree. And if they proceed to grant that degree without establishing appropriate standards, their certification will be a sham.

The most serious difficulty with college-wide requirements is not a matter of principle but of practice,
for too often they have been either instituted without
rational basis or perpetuated without adequate review. Instead of constructing integrated sequences in
the sciences, social sciences, and humanities that
would meet the needs of nonspecialists, many faculties have forced their students to choose almost
blindly from a wide group of courses structured
primarily with professional purposes in view.

What, for example, is a chemistry major to do if
he seeks an understanding of the social sciences but
is faced by countless courses on innumerable
specialized topics in anthropology, economics, geog-
raphy, government, psychology, and sociology? The
faculty in these disciplines should anticipate this
situation, pool their resources, and offer courses
specially designed to solve this problem.

Students should also be made aware that not all
courses offered by a single department are equally
appropriate for nonspecialists seeking a liberal education. For instance, "Emerson and Thoreau," "The
Plays of Synge," or "Science Fiction" are not adequate
substitutes for "Classics of World Literature," the
study of masterpieces by Homer, Dante, Shakespeare, and other literary titans. Indeed, asking an
uninformed student to decide for himself whether to
spend his limited time reading Dostoevsky or Jules
Verne is plainly irresponsible.

Not to be forgotten is that regulations regarding
requirements must exhibit common sense. A student
should be permitted to waive any requirement if he
can pass an equivalency examination, and appropriate credit should be awarded for analogous courses
taken at comparable institutions.

Of course, members of a college faculty will not

always agree about curricular details, but such disagreements also exist among members of law school and medical school faculties. Disputes of this sort are no reason to abandon all requirements, any more than disputes among legislators are reason to abolish all laws.

What is crucial is the constant reexamination of requirements, modifying them as wisely as possible in the light of changing social and intellectual conditions. No requirement should be sacrosanct. Each must repeatedly prove its value or be abandoned. But contrary to a view prevalent in recent years, modifying requirements does not necessarily imply lessening them. Sometimes what is needed is to augment them.

Chapter 12

The Faculty

Many readers who agree with the educational philosophy I have now presented may nevertheless doubt the practicality of assigning so much responsibility to members of the faculty. Such skepticism was expressed bluntly by one experienced teacher who wrote, "I have met few professors whom I would hire to run a peanut stand, let alone be the guardian of wisdom and Western civilization."[1]

Virtually anyone who has ever attended college can relate harrowing stories about incredible tribulations suffered at the hands of incompetent instructors. I myself have never forgotten my English composition teacher who lectured incoherently, failed to appear for scheduled office hours, and awarded no grade higher than C+. When one day in class he mentioned that another section of the same course had room for a few students, the news precipitated a stampede for the door.

But there is another side to the issue, for the faculty of the college I was privileged to attend included an extraordinary number of eminent scholars who were superb undergraduate teachers. Among them were Jacques Barzun, Daniel Bell, Donald Frame, Charles Frankel, Peter Gay, Moses Hadas, Gilbert Highet, Richard Hofstadter, Polykarp Kusch, Ernest Nagel, Meyer Schapiro, and Lionel Trilling. Surely it would not have been inappropriate to consider that esteemed group "the guardian of wisdom and Western civilization."

We cannot escape the fact that the quality of a school depends primarily upon the quality of its faculty. Neither concerned students nor an able administration can make the informed evaluations that lie at the heart of the educational process. Such judgments require expertise, and the faculty are supposed to be the experts. If they either lack the knowledge or lose the will to act responsibly, disaster is imminent.

No doubt every college would consider itself committed to maintaining the finest possible faculty. Why then are so many professors a disappointment to their colleagues and their students? One popular explanation for the poor quality of much college instruction is that faculty members are required to research as well as teach. And, it is said, when the rule is "publish or perish," pedants publish and teachers perish.

However, writing professional articles or books facilitates good teaching rather than hindering it, for such scholarly activity develops an individual's ability to think critically by leading him to formulate his thoughts with care and precision. Not every idea that sounds convincing in conversation can survive the

scrutiny that must be endured by the written word,
especially when the readers are experts.

A professor who, despite having studied his subject for many years, has nothing to say of any interest
to his peers, is unlikely to foster curiosity or imagination among his students. And an instructor whose
thinking is slipshod or shallow is not apt to persuade
his class of the importance of accuracy and thorough
workmanship. Granted that some outstanding
scholars are poor teachers and that some who have
published little are excellent teachers, nevertheless,
in Whitehead's words, "one good test for the general efficiency of a faculty is that as a whole it
shall be producing in published form its quota of
contributions of thought."[2]

We are often reminded of one great teacher who
wrote nothing: Socrates. But those who appeal to his
case tend to overlook that he spent his life in public
debate with the cleverest minds of his day, forcing
them to rethink their fundamental commitments. No
one would doubt the scholarly qualifications of any
contemporary philosopher who could do the same.
But, as Socrates himself pointed out, impressing
students and friends is no guarantee of one's
acumen.

Few who oppose the "publish or perish" principle
would object to the demand that faculty members
"think or perish"; yet to publish is only to make
available to all the results of one's best thinking. An
instructor who fails to do that must seek alternative
ways of providing clear and substantial evidence of
his intellectual vigor. If he is unable to shoulder the
burden of proof, others are justified in doubting the
quality of his thinking and, hence, of his teaching.[3]

Another common explanation for the disappointing quality of college instruction focuses on the practice of awarding professors tenure. Why, it is asked,

should anyone receive permanent job security? Do we not thereby pamper the indolent and protect the incompetent?

Unquestionably, the tenure system has its dangers, but none are so great as those that would attend its abandonment. For tenure has historically proven a bulwark of academic freedom, the right of professionally qualified persons to seek, teach, and publish the truth as they see it in their own fields of expertise.

Faculty members must be safeguarded against intimidation, for where it festers, the pursuit of knowledge is hampered and good teaching becomes a virtual impossibility. There have always been those both outside and inside the university who would stifle free inquiry in the name of some cause or other that supposedly demands everyone's unthinking allegiance. The justification of the tenure system is its critical role in the continuing battle that supporters of liberal education wage against such fanaticism.[4]

To defend the tenure system in principle, however, is not to applaud the ways it has been implemented. Surely most schools have awarded tenure far too liberally. An individual has not been required to demonstrate why he deserves tenure; instead, his institution has been expected to demonstrate why he doesn't. In court a person ought to be presumed innocent until proven guilty, but in matters of special skill one should not be supposed competent until so proven. A school's failure to observe this guideline results in a faculty encumbered with deadwood, and few departments have managed to avoid this unfortunate phenomenon. But to see how easily a mistake can be made, consider the following hypothetical but realistic case.

Adam Goodhart arrives at Podunk U. to begin his teaching career. During his first and second years he gains experience teaching standard departmental offerings while struggling with and finally finishing his dissertation, which he had optimistically estimated he would complete before his arrival. In his third and fourth years he devotes himself to planning several new courses and participating in an exciting interdisciplinary program. While reasonably successful as a teacher, he publishes two articles derived from his dissertation. In his fifth and sixth years he continues to enjoy good rapport with students while publishing a couple of book reviews and another article, this one based on a seminar paper written in graduate school. He has also begun working on what he hopes will be a book-length manuscript, but the project is still at a very early stage.

Thus at the end of six years, in accordance with the principles of the American Association of University Professors, Goodhart comes up for tenure. A decision must be made. He is liked by his students, has various publications, and is at work on a major scholarly project. He is a cooperative colleague and has participated enthusiastically in interdepartmental activities. Should he be awarded tenure?

Doing so involves excessive risk, for his most productive years may lie behind him. He has not clearly demonstrated the capacity for sustained, creative effort, and a careful examination of his bibliography raises serious doubts as to whether he has produced any significant scholarship since his dissertation. His good rapport with students may be based more on youthful enthusiasm and a spirit of cameraderie, probably short-lived, rather than on fundamental pedagogic skills and enduring qualities of mind that would sustain his teaching in later years. Visits to his classroom may even have raised some doubts in this direction. His contributions to the life of the college may decline when the novelty of such activities wanes, and as time goes on he may not even keep in close touch with the frontiers of his own subject. If he is awarded tenure and then fulfills our worst fears, those who suffer most will be the generations of students forced to endure his premature academic senility.

Of course, were he retained he might in the long run prove to be a significant asset to the university. But that is only a possibility, not a probability. And for the sake of future students as well as in the interest of each academic discipline, every effort should be made to appoint and retain only those individuals who, compared to all other available candidates, are most likely to achieve excellence. Adhering to such a rigorous standard is the surest way to avoid the succession of egregious and irremediable errors that are the inevitable consequence of laxity.

Those responsible for making tenure decisions should bear in mind Sidney Hook's observation that "most . . . tenured faculty who have lapsed into apparent professional incompetence . . . were marginal cases when their original tenure status was being considered, and reasons other than their proficiency as scholars and teachers were given disproportionate weight."[5] In short, the rule of thumb should be: when in doubt, say no.

But can nothing be done about those tenured professors whose gross incompetence has become an embarrassment to their colleagues and a menace to their students? Interestingly, the American Association of University Professors' own "Statement of Principles on Academic Freedom and Tenure" envisages the possibility of "termination for cause" and describes a procedure for "the hearing of charges of incompetence."[6] But hardly anyone, it seems, has ever been found guilty of such charges. Why not?

Understandably, faculty members and administrators are loath to brand an individual as an incompetent, thus publicly disgracing him and, in effect, forcing him out of the profession. Furthermore, conducting appropriate hearings involves an enormous amount of time, trouble, and expense, especially considering the endless appeals that are certain to ensue. And since neither judges nor juries are experts in the relevant subject areas, proving academic incompetence in a courtroom is no easy matter.

Nevertheless, schools should at least establish the machinery to carry out the hearing of charges of incompetence, and some procedures should be implemented to review regularly the work of all tenured professors. For the absence of such safeguards is no tribute to academic freedom but an invitation to academic irresponsibility.

Improving college teaching, however, is not only a matter of adjusting the practice of the tenure system. In addition, we need to recognize that most professors have never spent even a moment of their lives in formal study of the art of instruction. They have been forced to learn on the job, using their students as guinea pigs. Indeed, while it is normally assumed that an individual who applies for a position as a faculty member will hold a Ph.D. or its equivalent as proof of his scholarly competence, he is not usually expected to offer any evidence at all that he possesses the ability to teach.

Yet intellectual competence and pedagogic competence are two different qualities. One cannot be an outstanding teacher without thorough knowledge of subject matter, but to possess that knowledge does not guarantee the ability to communicate it to a student. And this ability is by no means easy to acquire. The number of great teachers is as small as the number of great artists or scientists. And just as an artist or scientist needs to master essential skills, so a teacher must do the same.

Admittedly, teaching college students is in some ways easier than teaching elementary-school students. Youngsters quickly indicate their boredom or disapproval by yelling or throwing chalk. Older students faced with poor teaching simply fall asleep. However, this reaction is in one respect quite unfortunate, since an elementary-school teacher is made immediately aware of his pedagogic inadequacy, while a college teacher may go on for years without ever realizing his ineptitude.

The most practical approach to the entire problem is for graduate schools to offer courses in methods of teaching and to require them of all students who are to be recommended for faculty appointments. These courses should involve future professors in discussing and practicing all phases of the teaching process, including motivating students, choosing materials, presenting lectures, guiding discussions, constructing examinations, and grading papers. The person selected to direct such a course ought himself to be a productive researcher and outstanding instructor, for he is in the best possible position to make clear to graduate students the scholarly and pedagogical responsibilities of a faculty member.[7]

No program of study can turn poor teachers into great ones. But if introduced by a distinguished mentor during those early years when individuals are most likely to welcome suggestions, it can turn inaudible lecturers into audible ones, disorganized seminar leaders into more organized ones, and careless graders into more careful ones. Most importantly, it can turn unreflective teachers into reflective ones, and that is the crucial step on the path toward the improvement of college teaching.

Conclusion

Throughout this work I have endeavored to bring to light the educational commitments implicit in the ideals of democracy. In particular, I have tried to show how freedom, individuality, and equality relate to discipline, authority, and excellence.

The most unhappy students I have ever known were those who found themselves in a leisurely atmosphere where they learned nothing, while the happiest were those experiencing the joy of surmounting high intellectual barriers. Ease soon brings boredom; challenge breeds interest and excitement.

A teacher should be sympathetic to anyone suffering the pains of genuine learning, but critical of those complacently putting forth less than their best effort. Even though attacks on examinations, grades, requirements, and standards may sometimes be justified, the proper response in such cases is to develop more useful examinations, more equitable grades, more appropriate requirements, and more sensible standards.

In sum, the success of a democratic community depends in great part upon the understanding and capability of its citizens. And in the complex world in which we live, to acquire sufficient understanding and capability requires a rigorous education. If we fail to provide that education, we shall have only ourselves to blame as our schools produce intellectual stagnation instead of contributing to a more vigorous and enlightened society.

NOTES

Introduction

1. *The Annotated Alice,* ed. Martin Gardner (Cleveland: World Publishing Co., 1960), p. 88.

Chapter 1   The Democratic Framework

1. *The Republic of Plato,* trans. Francis Macdonald Cornford (London: Oxford University Press, 1941), p. 558b.

2. *Intelligence in the Modern World: John Dewey's Philosophy,* ed. Joseph Ratner (New York: Modern Library, 1939), p. 402.

Chapter 2   The Content of a Liberal Education

1. Alfred North Whitehead, *The Aims of Education and Other Essays* (1929; rpt. New York: Free Press, 1967), p. 7.

2. Sidney Hook, *Education for Modern Man: A New Perspective* (New York: Alfred A. Knopf, 1963), pp. 203, 207.

Chapter 3   Schools

1. Alexis de Tocqueville, *Democracy in America,* 2 vols. (1835; rpt. New York: Vintage Books, 1960).

Chapter 4   The Myth of the Royal Road

1. Jacques Barzun, *The House of Intellect* (New York: Harper & Brothers, 1959), p. 112.

2. John Dewey, *Democracy and Education* (1916; rpt. New York: Free Press, 1966), p. 129.

Chapter 5   The Art of Instruction

1. Hook, pp. 230-231.
2. Whitehead, p. 36.
3. The college instructor who so inspired me was Professor James P. Shenton of Columbia College.

Chapter 6   Excellence

1. Charles A. Reich, *The Greening of America* (New York: Random House, 1970), pp. 226-227.

2. An illuminating discussion of these matters can be found in Paul Edwards' *The Logic of Moral Discourse* (New York: Free Press, 1955).

3. Barzun, p. 197.

Chapter 7   The Case for Examinations and Grades

1. Grade designations, however, are few in number and have a relatively standardized meaning. Therefore, teachers who use them idiosyncratically are not the victims of linguistic ambiguity but of pedagogic inadequacy.

2. The currently explosive issue of "open admissions" would be defused if the open door swung, as it should, out as well as in.

Chapter 8   The Case against Examinations and Grades

1. Whitehead, p. 34.

2. These five levels of work are commonly symbolized by the letters: A, B, C, D, F. Teachers who misuse these symbols are an educational menace; their sins are discussed in the next chapter.

3. Gilbert Highet, *The Art of Teaching* (1950; rpt. New York: Random House, 1954), p. 132.

Chapter 9   Testing and Grading

1. One method of encouraging teachers not to overgrade is for transcripts to include both a student's course grade and the average grade of all students in that course. In this way grade inflation would at least be publicly exposed.

Chapter 10   The Authority of a Teacher

1. Donald H. Naftulin, M.D., John E. Ware, Jr., and Frank A. Donnelly, "The Doctor Fox Lecture: A Paradigm of Educational Seduction," *Journal of Medical Education,* 48 (1973), 630-635. Only one of the groups heard Dr. Fox in person; the other two were shown a videotape of the original session.

2. Charles Frankel, *Education and the Barricades* (New York: W. W. Norton & Co., 1968), pp. 30-31.

Chapter 11   Requirements

1. *New York University Bulletin: Washington Square College of Arts and Sciences,* 1965-1966 (New York: New York University, 1965), p. 30.

2. *Columbia University Bulletin: Columbia College,* 1960-1961 (New York: Columbia University, 1960), pp. 36, 59, 66, 96-97.

3. John Stuart Mill, *On Liberty* (Indianapolis: Bobbs-Merrill, 1956), p. 76.

4. Students seeking to influence decisions regarding curriculum and related matters should be encouraged to present their views to appropriate faculty committees, but not offered the right to vote on these issues which can only be reasonably decided by experts.

Chapter 12   The Faculty

1. Professor X, *This Beats Working For a Living: The Dark Secrets of a College Professor* (New Rochelle, N. Y.: Arlington House, 1973), p.11.

2. Whitehead, p. 99.

3. Members of a graduate faculty are, of course, expected to make even greater contributions to the development of their discipline.

4. A school's commitment to academic freedom is also incompatible with its adopting any official stance on issues unrelated to its educational ideals. Free inquiry is impeded when certain opinions have been officially declared false and others true. Whether a philosophical argument is sound or a war immoral is a matter for discussion, not decree.

5. Sidney Hook, *Education & the Taming of Power* (La Salle, Ill.: Open Court, 1973), p. 213.

6. "Academic Freedom and Tenure: 1940 Statement of Principles and Interpretive Comments," *AAUP Bulletin,* 60 (1974), 270.

7. A book intended to supplement such courses is Steven M. Cahn, ed., *Scholars Who Teach: The Art of College Teaching* (Chicago: Nelson-Hall, 1978).

INDEX

Academic honors, grades and, 52

Achievement: grades as a measure of, 50-51; levels of, in grading, 72-73

Acton, Lord, quoted, 5

Aesthetics, sensitivity to, 9

Alice's Adventures in Wonderland (Carroll), quoted, xi

American Association of University Professors, 99, 100

Aristotle, 10

BA degree, requirements for the, 85-93

Barzun, Jacques, 96; quoted, 22, 39

Bell, Daniel, 96

Bunker, Archie, 2

Chess, teaching, 25-26

Clarification in teaching, 30-31

Competence, students as judges of, 80-82

Competition, grades as fostering, 58-59

Complexity of academic subjects, 30

Creativity, testing as a limit to, 55-56

Curriculum, faculty responsibility for a structured, 91-93

Curve, grading on the, 74-75

Declaration of Independence, 39

Degrees: function of academic, 19-20; granting college, 51-52; requirements for, 85-93

Democracy, Plato's critique of, 3-4

Dewey, John, quoted, 5, 24

Eclipse of Excellence (Cahn), ix

Education, definition of, 1

Educational requirements, 85-93

ABOUT THE AUTHOR

Steven M. Cahn is Professor of Philosophy and Chairman of the Department at the University of Vermont. Previously, he taught at Dartmouth College, Vassar College, the University of Rochester, and at New York University, where he chaired the Washington Square College Educational Policy Committee.

Born in Springfield, Massachusetts, in 1942, Dr. Cahn was graduated from Columbia College in 1963 and received his Ph.D. from Columbia University in 1966. The author of four books and editor of six, his articles have appeared in such varied publications as *The Encyclopedia of Philosophy, The New York Times, The American Journal of Medicine, Learning and the Law*, and *The Journal of Aesthetics and Art Criticism*. He is a member of Phi Beta Kappa and has been a consultant to the National Endowment for the Humanities.